Minidragons:

FRAGILE ECONOMIC MIRACLES IN THE PACIFIC

Harry C. Trexler Library
Muhlenberg College

Mini Dragons

FRAGILE ECONOMIC MIRACLES IN THE PACIFIC

Steven M. Goldstein, Editor

Ambrose Video Publishing

NEW YORK

Westview Press

BOULDER • SAN FRANCISCO • OXFORD

MINIDRAGONS: FRAGILE ECONOMIC MIRACLES IN THE PACIFIC
is a project of Contemporary Learning Systems of East Lansing, Inc., in association with
Maryland Public Television, and is funded by Ambrose Video Publishing, Inc.

CONTEMPORARY LEARNING SYSTEMS OF EAST LANSING, INC.

Dr. George A. Colburn, Director of Operations

David Kennard, Consultant, Television Productions

Jane L. Scheiber, Director of Education Programs

Dr. John Ball, Administrator, Publications Office

Judy O'Connor, Editorial Associate

Amina Tirana, Research Associate

MARYLAND PUBLIC TELEVISION

Leo Eaton, Senior Vice-President, Executive-in-Charge of Production

AMBROSE VIDEO PUBLISHING, INC.

William V. Ambrose, President

Cover and book design by Tom Gould

Published in 1991 in the United States of America by Ambrose Video Publishing, Inc., Suite 2245,
1290 Avenue of the Americas, New York, New York 10104, and by Westview Press, Inc., 5500 Central
Avenue, Boulder, Colorado 80301, and in the United Kingdom by Westview Press, 36 Lonsdale Road,
Summertown, Oxford OX2 7EW

Library of Congress Cataloging-in-Publication Data
Goldstein, Steven M. (Steven Martin)
Minidragons: fragile economic miracles in the Pacific
Steven M. Goldstein
1. East Asia—Economic policy.   2. East Asia—Politics and government.
3. Economic forecasting—East Asia.   I. Title.
Hc460.5G65   1991   90-28787
338.95—dc20   CIP
ISBN 0-8133-8257-2
ISBN 0-8133-1264-7(trade pbk.)
ISBN 0-8133-8258-0(text pbk.)

Printed and bound in the United States of America

10 9 8 7 6 5 4 3 2 1

Contents

FOR DAN

Preface

The purpose of this book is to introduce one of the most significant international developments of the post World War II era—the dramatic socio-economic transformation achieved by Hong Kong, Singapore, South Korea and Taiwan. In less than three decades, these "minidragons" of Asia have become major economic players, not only in the economy of the Pacific rim, but in the global economic system as well. In the essays which follow, the nature of this transformation is charted; its causes are described; and some assessment is made of the factors that will shape the future of these "fragile economic miracles."

This volume was originally conceived as a companion to the television series entitled *Minidragons,* an international co-production of Maryland Public Television (MPT) with NHK, Japan, and Film Australia. Aired in the United States via PBS, this four part series presents to a wider audience the dimensions and global implications of the changes brought about by these economic powers. Leo Eaton, Senior Vice-President for National and International Production at MPT, actively promoted the concept of a major book by Pacific Rim scholars. William V. Ambrose of Ambrose Video Publishing, Inc., distributor of the video cassettes for the series, provided funding so the project could be carried out by Contemporary Learning Systems, Inc. (CLS).

Thanks must go to several people who assisted in the production of this volume. First of all, I am indebted to the authors of the country studies who endured short deadlines and numerous edits to produce excellent works of scholarship. Pamela White, who served as copy-editor demonstrated, as always, an extra-ordinary combination of meticulousness, skill and—most of all—patience. John Ball proved to be a cheerful and very astute manager of the overall editing and technical preparation of this book while Shoshanna Korn provided quick and reliable research assistance. Susan McEachern of Westview Press gave essential support and advice in seeing this project through to its present, published form. My wife Erika deserves thanks—even though she says she doesn't. Finally, recognition must go to George Colburn, founder and president of CLS, who organized this project and oversaw its development. He has, once more, proven to be a provocative and stimulating colleague in projects linking documentary television with publications of value both to the general public and the academic community.

SMG
Florence, Massachusetts
February, 1991

The Minidragons:
Economic Miracles and Political Change

Steven M.
Goldstein

I n describing the postwar development of Taiwan, Singapore, Hong Kong, and South Korea, it is difficult to resist using the term "miracle." The scope and speed of the political and economic transformations in these countries have startled a generation of observers. Less than three decades ago the four would have received no more than a footnote in discussions of the global economy. Today they wield significant economic influence, and their developmental strategies are closely studied for lessons that might generate similar successes elsewhere.

Yet to the extent that "miracle" connotes an accident or the intervention of some divine providence, it seems a particularly inappropriate term for these dramatic changes. In most of these societies the recent transformations didn't just happen; they were carefully crafted by business and political leaders. Moreover, as the 1990's begin it is clear that these achievements might well lack another quality often associated with miracles—permanence. All of the minidragons are facing severe political and economic challenges that they must overcome if they are to carry their successes into the future.

Understanding the Minidragons

Why should the evolution of these societies be of concern to us? The obvious answer is that as a group they constitute an important component of the world economy. How they deal with future challenges will have a significant impact on that global system and, through it, on all of us. However, there is another, more fundamental, reason for seeking to understand the changes in these countries.

In the decades since the end of the Second World War, Taiwan, Singapore, Hong Kong, and South Korea have each experienced an industrial revolution, but they have done so in a different era, in a different world, and within different socio-

Steven M. Goldstein teaches political science at Smith College. His field of specialty is Chinese politics and foreign policy. He has written widely on issues ranging from Sino-American relations to the development of the Communist movement in China. His most recent books are *Single Sparks: China's Rural Revolutions* and *The Chinese Adapting the Past, Building the Future*.

Notes for this chapter can be found on pages 183–184.

political contexts, compared with the industrial revolution in Europe and the United States. For more than a century the industrial revolution of the West was considered to represent a paradigm—it was *the* industrial revolution. With the transformation of Japan the revolution moved eastward. And now, in the minidragons, we have a group of societies that have undergone an analogous process.

What insights into the nature of (and requisites for) industrialization do their experiences provide? Going further, what can we learn about the diverse forms that industrialization can take in the Asian context? More specifically, is it any more proper to homogenize the courses taken by these four states by using the term "minidragons" than it would be to lump together Prussian Junkers, Manchester industrialists, and American robber barons into something called the "Western industrial revolution?"

In short, the four minidragons exhibit variations upon two themes. The first: collectively, they reflect an Asian version of the global industrial revolution that began in eighteenth-century England. The second: individually, each presents a quite distinctive variant of that version.

A discussion of the first theme is a useful corrective to the assumption that a Western phenomenon of two hundred years ago represented a universal process. Addressing the second counteracts the tendency to overemphasize the similarities among these states, a tendency reflected in the common use of such collective terms as "the Gang of Four," "the Four Tigers," or even "the Minidragons." What emerges from the chapters in this book are not simply remarkable sagas of four countries, but also a contribution to the understanding of the complex pattern of similarities and differences that characterize their experiences.

The Common Thread:
Rapid and Adaptable Outward-Looking Growth

The most obvious shared characteristic of these four societies is their remarkable economic growth in the decades since World War II. In the 1950's Hong Kong was an overcrowded British colony seeking to absorb a flood of refugees fleeing the communist victory in China. At the same time on Taiwan, the defeated remnants of Chiang Kai-shek's Nationalist forces were struggling to establish a viable base for a seemingly quixotic return to the mainland. In South Korea in 1959, the leaders of a military coup were confronting a legacy of war and political corruption. Finally, in 1965, the tiny city of Singapore was confronting the unexpected and unwanted independence that followed a failed union with Malaysia. Only the foolhardy would have predicted that all these societies would soon be dramatically transformed.

Yet this transformation is precisely what has occurred. From 1965 to 1986 Taiwan rose from its position as twenty-eighth largest exporter in the world to tenth, South Korea from thirty-third to thirteenth. It has been predicted that between 1986 and 1992 the volume of exports from all four minidragons will grow by 135% against a growth of 20% in Latin America and 46% worldwide. Their domestic growth has been just as remarkable. In the early 1980's Hong Kong's real Gross Domestic Product was growing at an average annual rate of 5.8%, Taiwan's at 6.2%, Singapore's at 6.5%, and South Korea's at 7.6%. During the same period the Japanese economy grew at an average annual rate of 2.3%, the American economy at 2.4%.

In 1988 the per capita shares of Gross National Product in South Korea, Taiwan, Hong Kong, and Singapore were $3,436, $4,837, $8,158, and $8,817 respectively. Elsewhere in Asia per capita GNP ranged from almost $2,018 in Malaysia to $527 in the Philippines. More importantly, studies suggest that income distribution is more equitable in the four minidragons than it is in Latin America (save Cuba) or the United States.

In short, whether judged against the industrial West, Latin America, or their neighbors in Asia, these societies have performed prodigious economic feats—and all of this in a combined area about the size of Arkansas which, while enjoying comparatively little in the way of natural resources, sustains some of the highest population densities in the world.

In 1987 the World Bank published a study which classified forty-three developing countries according to their foreign trade strategies, which were ranked from "strongly outward oriented" to "strongly inward oriented." The first category contained South Korea, Hong Kong, and Singapore (Taiwan, which would also have been listed among this group, is not included in World Bank statistics). This classification is clearly substantiated by the proportion of foreign trade to gross domestic product in these states: 37% in South Korea, 52% in Taiwan, 117% in Hong Kong and 195% in Singapore. So the four minidragons not only share a record of unusual economic growth, but they have achieved that growth in a distinctive way—through heavy reliance on exports.

Economists call such a developmental strategy "Export Oriented Industrialization" (EOI) and differentiate it from "Import Substituting Industrialization" (ISI). As one commentator has noted:

> The labels convey content: ISI sought to promote growth by shielding national economies from the gale-force winds of international competition so as to nurture infant industries to adult maturity; EOI fueled internal growth by producing directly for international markets with little or no domestic consumption of the products produced.

These categories are, of course, not necessarily mutually exclusive. As we shall see, Taiwan and South Korea still protect their domestic economies even as they produce for export. However, based largely on the experience of the minidragons, many economists have argued that producing for foreign rather than domestic markets is a preferable developmental strategy for newly developing countries. Why this is so is by no means certain. One reason is surely the natural limitations on production imposed by domestic markets. Moreover, some observers point to the fact that while an inward orientation can promote such negative phenomena as protectionism, price distortions, and inflation, an outward orientation brings quicker payoffs and, through the pressures of international competition, promotes efficiency while reducing price distortions. Whatever the reasons, the success of an export-oriented strategy is apparent in the rapid economic growth that has characterized Taiwan, Singapore, Hong Kong, and South Korea.

These societies have shown more than the ability to achieve rapid growth, however. They have also demonstrated the capacity to sustain that growth, through a series of adaptations to changed domestic and international circumstances. Over the past three decades they have moved from strategy to strategy, orientation to orientation, to sustain their pattern of growth.

Singapore, Taiwan, and South Korea all began the process of industrialization with policies of import substitution, only to abandon that orientation in the mid-1960's. In Singapore, the failure of union with Malaysia made ISI impossible. Taiwan and South Korea abandoned ISI because of American pressure, and because of a growing awareness of the natural limits of an inward-oriented policy. The one exception, Hong Kong, moved right to EOI by drawing on trade-oriented entrepreneurial talent and capital from the Chinese mainland, particularly cosmopolitan Shanghai. By the mid-1960's, despite their dissimilar sizes, resource bases, historical backgrounds, and early industrial experiences, all four of the minidragons seemed to have come out at the same place: they were all pursuing a strategy of EOI based on labor-intensive light industry, with textiles and clothing dominating the export effort in all cases but Singapore.

However, EOI based on the labor-intensive manufacture of light industrial items proved, like ISI, to have a limited lifespan. By the 1970's full employment had driven up wages, suggesting that industrialization based on cheap labor might not be sustainable. Moreover, the international economic uncertainties created both by "oil shocks" and by growing protectionism in the West radically changed the international atmosphere. Faced with declining profits in traditional items, the movement of foreign businesses into yet cheaper labor markets in Asia, and resistance in foreign markets to many of the staples of earlier industrialization, all of the minidragons reoriented their economies during the 1970's and 1980's.

Singapore's economy moved in two directions. It developed technologically more sophisticated—and presumably more profitable—industries such as electronic components, pharmaceuticals, office machinery, and telecommunications equipment. At the same time Singapore developed its financial and business service sectors in the hope that it would become a regional center for international banking and trade in Southeast Asia. Hong Kong took a somewhat different route. Although the more internationalist orientation of post-Mao China stimulated growth in Hong Kong's trade and banking sectors similar to Singapore's, in manufacturing Hong Kong did not stray very far from the profile which it had maintained since the 1950's—labor-intensive manufacturing centered around garments and textiles.

In Taiwan and South Korea the second stage of EOI saw more radical departures from earlier patterns. In Taiwan there was dramatic growth in shipbuilding capacity (it became the fourth largest in the world) and some talk of developing an auto industry. But the two major areas targeted for development in Taiwan were heavy industry, such as petrochemicals that would serve traditional exports like plasticware and textiles, and exports in electronics and computers. By the end of the 1980's electronics had replaced clothing as the island's leading export. South Korea made the most radical shift as its economy abruptly moved into high technology, transportation, and heavy industry during the 1980's. From 1970 to 1981 minimal or negative growth in labor-intensive light industry stood in stark contrast to growth in exports in the transportation sector (which grew nearly tenfold) as well as in chemicals and electrical machinery (which both doubled). In only a decade South Korea had become a major shipbuilding, auto exporting, and high-tech power in the world economy.

The conclusion to be drawn is obvious: as remarkable as the speed of their growth is the apparent nimbleness with which the economies of the minidragons have transformed themselves in response to opportunities and constraints at home and abroad. There are, of course, several explanations for this adaptability. The essays that follow suggest that in at least three of these societies, one factor overshadows the rest—the powerful and intrusive economic role of the state.

The State and Economic Growth

The Interventionist State

From the vantage point of 1991, such a crediting of state intervention might seem anomalous. As socialist states in Eastern Europe rush to abandon planned economies, many in the West are quick to claim a victory for the free market over state regulation and for democracy over authoritarianism—a victory, in other words, of precisely those principles that are thought to lie at the core of the Anglo-

American model. But does this version of history square with the experiences of the minidragons?

There are no easy answers. Looking to the past, we see that nondemocratic, intrusive states have been prominent forces in the East Asian economic landscape. Unlike the experience of failure in the states of Eastern Europe, such state intrusion in Asia has brought economic success. Yet as we look to the minidragons' future, the continuance of past patterns seems problematic. Pressures are building in each of the four to make the state more accessible to the people and the economy more amenable to market forces. As has been the case with so much of their developmental experience, we see the minidragons elaborating on the Western path even as they display distinctive patterns among themselves.

Take the contrast between South Korea and Hong Kong. Soon after taking power the military leaders who overthrew Syngman Rhee established a pattern whereby the South Korean state intervened freely in the economic life of the country. Its broad repertoire of policies included state ownership of key industries, protective tariffs, export subsidies, management of investment through control of the banking system, and the creation of the large trading and manufacturing conglomerates known as *chaebol*. Indeed, one scholar has concluded that "every major shift in the industrial diversification of the decades of the 1960's and 1970's was instigated by the state." Outside of the Marxist-Leninist planned economies, few economies have departed further than South Korea's from the principles of *laissez-faire* capitalism.

On the other hand, Hong Kong's economy appears to epitomize *laissez-faire* principles. In the 1950's, the colony benefited from the influx of considerable entrepreneurial talent and capital from the mainland. For the past three decades Hong Kong has stuck to a pattern "characterized by a high dependence on small and adaptable entrepreneurs to find new business opportunities and a minimal involvement of government in direct production." This minimal state intervention has included such actions as the provision of infrastructural services, management of the crucial real estate market, and, on rare occasions, the establishment of advisory committees to promote selected exports such as textiles or electronics. There was some talk in the late 1970's of a greater role for government under the rubric of "positive nonintervention." However, the government owns no industry, provides no control over capital flows, maintains no central bank, subsidizes no industries, and establishes no wage controls. Of course one should not minimize the crucial importance of the state in Hong Kong in providing a stable political environment for economic development—a role which has become more important in recent years. In its own distinctive way, the British colonial government has played a central role in the economic transformation of Hong Kong.

Still, the fact remains that the Hong Kong pattern sharply contrasts with the pattern of governmental intervention, not only in South Korea, but also in Taiwan and Singapore. While less intrusive than the South Korean government, the state in Taiwan and Singapore has nonetheless played an essential role in promoting economic development using similar interventionist techniques.

Unlike the socialist states, the presence of a strong state in these East Asian societies does not exclude private enterprise. The private sector exists in all four countries, although differing in size and composition. The South Korean economy is dominated by the *chaebol,* large and diversified conglomerates with familiar names like Hyundai and Samsung whose sales in recent years have equalled two-thirds of the nation's GNP. In contrast, in Taiwan the government has about a 20% share in manufacturing, and the private sector is dominated by small, family-based firms—in 1981, 80% of Taiwanese firms employed fewer than twenty persons. Hong Kong is closer to the Taiwanese model of small firms. Singapore has followed a very different path; the domestic bourgeoisie started from a very small base and has remained a secondary force squeezed between a highly managerial state and influential foreign corporations.

Why have such state-dominated economies been so effective? Many observers believe it is precisely their nondemocratic nature. All of the states of the mini-dragons fit the description "soft-authoritarian." Until very recently none has had true multi-party systems or truly competitive elections. Indeed, Hong Kong is still ruled as a Crown colony of Great Britain. Yet many would argue that this nondemocratic environment is an advantage, for it has insulated the leadership in these countries from societal forces that might have diluted, or even prevented, the radical changes of recent years. Leaders who are forced to build societal coalitions or placate different power bases—labor, farmers, landholders—are often too vulnerable to embark on the sometimes unpopular policies needed to fuel rapid, export-oriented growth.

There are, of course, other elements that make up a strong state. After all, history offers ample evidence of leaders of nondemocratic states who have plundered their nations rather than developed them. But this has not been the case in these four societies. The minidragons appear also to have benefited from farsighted political leaders who, although they have not always been benevolent or made correct policy choices, have pushed their nations towards development. Indeed, one leader, Lee Kuan Yew of Singapore, has guided his country since its independence in 1965, presiding over a powerful and unified governing elite as well as a well-staffed and usually honest bureaucracy.

Understanding the complex role of the state in East Asia and its interaction with an often vibrant private sector has not been an easy task for outside analysts. What is the secret of the successful coexistence of the state with the market and private enterprise? How could these economies have done so well despite the fact that the intrusiveness of the state seems to violate fundamental precepts of neoclassical *laissez-faire* capitalism? Why have these states succeeded where those in Eastern Europe appear to have failed?

Some economists have argued that the difference between the two cases is that in Taiwan, Singapore, and South Korea the state has "gotten it right," intervening in ways that would promote rather than inhibit domestic entrepreneurial talents and market forces. The purpose of the government in these countries, according to this view, "is not to replace the market but to make the market work better and faster." Recently this argument has been challenged by other analysts who have noted that the protective tariffs, import subsidies, and currency controls of these countries can hardly be depicted as market-conforming. The issue is by no means settled. However, it is clear that the experience of the minidragons has prompted a reconsideration of Western *laissez-faire* assumptions about the role of state intervention in domestic economic development.

The Foreign Sector and the State

The success of the minidragons has also prompted some rethinking of the role of the foreign sector in late-developing countries. Most elites of newly industrializing countries view the industrial powers of the world with considerable ambivalence. While advanced nations can provide the capital and technology needed for economic transformation, they can manipulate such support to shape growth in ways that benefit themselves rather than the industrializing hosts. This view, known as "dependency theory," has been used by some analysts to explain the developmental difficulties of Latin America. However, when we look at the minidragons, it is clear that foreign participation has not necessarily led to either distorted growth or exploitation.

Part of the reason is that most of these countries can raise considerable investment capital at home because of their unusually high rates of savings. In 1986 their savings rates ranged from one and one-half to two and one-half times that of the United States. All four also look abroad for international financing and investment, but they do so to different degrees and in different ways. In this case the extremes are Hong Kong and Singapore. Although Hong Kong permits foreign investment with almost no controls, foreign capital has not been a major factor in either industrial development or capital formation. Both have drawn instead on local savings generated through banks in the colony. At the other extreme is Singapore, which has relied extraordinarily heavily on the international economic community to promote industrial growth. Foreign capital has come to Singapore not as much through loans as through direct investment by foreigners. In 1984 only 24% of businesses in Singapore were foreign owned, yet these enterprises produced 82% of direct exports, 62% of capital expenditures, and 53% of employment.

Unlike Hong Kong and Singapore, South Korea has been enormously resistant to foreign investment—but not to foreign borrowing. Outside of Japan, no other country in Asia has a lower rate of foreign direct investment in its economy. South Korea has the highest foreign debt of all the minidragons, however, with the state doing the borrowing and then apportioning out the proceeds among corporations. Between 1968 and 1984 the nation's foreign indebtedness grew from $1.2 billion to $43 billion, while debt as percentage of GNP grew from 0.8% to 7%. This policy stands in sharp contrast to Taiwan's, where the government has used domestic savings to limit foreign borrowing, at the same time funnelling foreign direct investment into selected, mostly high-tech, areas through the development of industrial parks and export zones.

The experiences of South Korea, Taiwan, and, to a lesser extent, Singapore, bring us back to the crucial role of the state. By closely regulating borrowing and investment, each of these governments has carefully managed and monitored foreign participation in the economy. The state has thus not only been a central driving force behind the rapid and adaptive growth of the past, but it has also played a major role in assuring that the international sector serves the goals of society rather than those of the borrowers or lenders.

Explaining Past Successes

For other nations seeking to emulate the minidragons (and for social scientists seeking to understand them), there is one final, but very important, question: What factors have contributed to their past successes? Analysts who stress the contribution of strong and politically insulated states often look to culture and history to explain the emergence of such states. All of the minidragons, after all, have been influenced by the tenets of Confucian culture. This body of thought originated in China, but eventually spread throughout Asia. It emphasizes the importance of a protective and benevolent state, honest leadership, and mass deference to authority. Because it describes many of the qualities of these states and cultivates frugality and hard work by the population, a number of commentators believe that Confucianism provides the key to the "Eastasia edge."

Others look to the more immediate past to explain both the emergence of strong states and the nature of the policies which they have implemented. Some commentators point to the colonial history of the minidragons. In this view British colonialism provided both Hong Kong and Singapore with an *entrepot* infrastructure and a trained civil service. In South Korea and Taiwan the Japanese supplied infrastructure as well as the example of a strong and interventionist developmental state. Still other analysts seeking to identify the sources of the minidragons' success have pointed variously to the limited resource bases that forced them to look abroad for economic growth and to the impact of historical developments which weakened the political power of major social groups such as labor, landowners, and the bourgeoisie.

Another influence in conditioning the development of successful economic policies has been the international environment. Commentators have pointed to the "flying goose" phenomenon in East Asia: the adoption of similar policies by the countries of the region. The influence of the postwar Japanese miracle of state-directed, export-driven growth has been unmistakable. There has also been the matter of what Stephan Haggard has called "international shocks." Each of these societies began its development with a crisis—in Taiwan, defeat; in Singapore, separation; in Hong Kong, a refugee influx; and in South Korea, war—that compelled it to address its economic problems. The international system has also contributed in more positive ways. South Korea and Taiwan in particular have received large amounts of American aid and advice which have promoted export-oriented growth. Finally, many observers have noted that all these societies had the good fortune to embark upon their expansionist policies at a time when the international economy was booming and industrialized countries provided open and eager markets.

These, then, are some of the factors that have been offered to explain the developmental success of the minidragons. A recurring theme of this introduction has been to question the tendency to lump these societies together. Attempts to explain past policies should not be exempt from such skepticism. No single factor explains the success of these societies, and the permutations of the explanatory factors that seem most influential differ from case to case. In the chapters that follow, we shall find that the reasons for the developmental courses taken by these countries are as diverse as the policies the chapters endeavor to explain.

Looking to the Future

After observing the early stages of the French Revolution, the eighteenth-century British commentator Edmund Burke proposed a law of politics: "A state without the means of some change," he asserted, "is without the means of its conservation." Almost two hundred years later, this statement is a succinct explanation for the past successes of the minidragons. However, it is an equally succinct summary of the challenges which they will confront in the future.

The "means of some change" in these countries have been very much in evidence since the Second World War. We have already noted the extraordinary manner in which the economies of these societies have both grown and changed direction in the face of changing international opportunities and domestic capabilities. At the same time, and perhaps as a precondition, political systems too have been adapted, even transformed, to confront new tasks. The most striking example is how the militarily bankrupt Nationalist regime in Taiwan changed itself into a strong force for development. Even in Hong Kong, where the government has been the least interventionist, British authorities did a remarkable job maintaining civil peace and a stable investment climate as the colony was transformed from a sleepy trading outpost of imperialism into a bustling manufacturing center and *entrepot*.

As we enter the 1990's, pressures for change are developing once more. In the international economic realm, conditions are moving further away from the very propitious environment established in the 1960's. Alongside such perennial short-term factors as international business cycles, political crises, and the constant struggle to develop new products and markets, more long-term and ominous trends are developing. Protectionism is on the rise in many of the industrial nations, especially in the United States, a major market for the minidragons. Western protectionism is a problem for all of the minidragons, but it is a particular issue for Taiwan and South Korea. These countries have based their growth on free access to foreign markets even as they have limited foreign access to their own markets through protective tariffs, exchange rate controls, and foreign investment regulations. During the late 1980's serious crises have been averted through patient negotiation on both sides; however, the danger of protectionism persists, and if its effects are to be controlled, then many of the minidragons will have to rethink past policies regarding foreign access to their own economies.

There is also pressure from other countries with larger and cheaper labor forces (Thailand and the People's Republic of China [PRC], for example) which are threatening to erode the competitiveness of the minidragons' still important labor-intensive sectors. Recent figures suggest that manufacturing for export is lagging as the leading factor in economic growth in certain of the minidragons. In response, governments are considering shifts in economic policy comparable to those in the 1970's. Their alternatives range from aggressive development of new product lines to the importation of workers to the shifting of their own investment abroad where there are cheaper labor markets. In this vein it is striking that Taiwanese investors are looking to the mainland even as Singapore looks to Indonesia and Malaysia. The minidragons, which once thrived on investment from abroad, are paradoxically now becoming foreign investors themselves. These states appear once again to be on the verge of taking some radically new economic directions in the face of a changing international environment.

And so we return to Edmund Burke. The minidragons are being challenged yet again to make economic changes essential to the continuation of the economic miracles of the past. A major factor facilitating past changes was a strong and stable state. Yet as the minidragons enter the 1990's, the very governments that engineered past changes are now themselves confronting the need to change. Should they fail to do so, the future viability of these economies will surely be endangered.

The heart of the political problem is quite simple: old political formulas are being questioned. In Taiwan, Singapore, and South Korea, for example, the notion of an interventionist state is being challenged from several quarters. Many of the international agencies and advisory bodies that earlier had been supportive of such intervention now seem to be pressing for less intrusion by the state and greater privatization. They are joined in this call by bureaucratic and middle-class voices seeking an end to tight government control. Naturally such pressures for change—from both without and within—do not go unchallenged by defenders of the status quo. Bureaucrats accustomed to managing the economy are understandably reluctant to relinquish their power and influence; as one commentator recently noted, "the hardest thing for economic policy makers is to unlearn the lessons of the past." The larger economic interests that have benefited from governmental bailouts and special favors are showing a similar reluctance to be cut loose. In Hong Kong the situation differs somewhat from that in the other minidragons. Here the existing *laissez-faire* structure seems threatened by plans for the imposition in 1997 of a Chinese bureaucracy committed to strong state intervention in the economy. In short, in all of these societies the political consensus and bureaucratic unity that lay at the heart of past policies are clearly eroding.

However, the most significant changes occurring in these states lie at the nexus of state and society. As we have seen, all of these societies have been ruled by authoritarian systems whose elites have been insulated from socio-political pressures. This lack of accountability is often credited with giving the leaders of these states the freedom to make the sudden changes in direction that have characterized policy in the past. Recent developments in all of the minidragons suggest that this core element in the political system is now being seriously challenged by increasingly vocal societies demanding that policies be responsive to their particular specific needs rather than to some abstract notion of national economic growth.

As the following chapters suggest, the voices calling most loudly for change are those of the middle classes chafing under the political and economic restrictions of these authoritarian regimes. However, broader societal groups such as labor and farmers are also joining the fray. In Taiwan the local populace, joined by middle-class mainlanders, is demanding a greater voice in a government long dominated by an aging mainland elite. The South Korean government is faced with a growing labor movement and an awakening agricultural lobby. In Hong Kong the specter of incorporation into the PRC has stimulated a broadly based attempt to replace the undemocratic British colonial rule before 1997 with a more popular government better able to protect the population from the government in Beijing. Even in quiescent Singapore, middle-class dissatisfaction, labor unrest, and ethnic tensions are all having a political impact. Although the electoral system has assured the dominance of the ruling People's Action Party, the party's total popular vote has slipped to 62%.

Probably the most impressive political adaptation has taken place in Taiwan, where since the middle 1980's the ruling elite has gradually opened the system up to allow greater and more regularized activities by the opposition. In South Korea the decision in 1987 to hold elections and the recent merger of the ruling party with two opposition groups has proven to be a much more fractious process, the outcome of which remains uncertain. Even the British colonial authorities have responded to broad social pressures and granted a limited number of elective offices in Hong Kong's legislative body. However, this unprecedented action seems to many in the colony a halfway measure intended to satisfy popular concerns while allaying the PRC's fears that London is legislating for what will soon be Chinese territory. Of the four countries Singapore is clinging most tenaciously to the belief that opposition is fundamentally disruptive to society; however, the formal retirement of Lee Kuan Yew, the man who has guided the nation with an iron hand since 1959, and the coming to power of a second generation of leaders, have precipitated the most critical political juncture in the nation's twenty-five-year history. In short, although governments in all these societies have responded to some degree to demands for change, the future of peaceful political change in the minidragons is anything but certain.

It is appropriate to close this introduction by reflecting on the permanence of miracles. The industrial revolution in the West was accompanied by poverty, depression, social tensions, and war, all of which challenged, and sometimes toppled, social orders. After three decades of startling change, the minidragons confront the shades of some similar perils today. As late developers they were able

to learn from the West and perform in a few decades economic feats that took Western societies centuries to accomplish. In doing so, they have benefited from a remarkable political stability that promoted and protected that growth. Now that stability can no longer be taken for granted. States that have performed economic miracles in the past are now confronted with the necessity of performing political miracles if they are to continue to build on their accomplishments.

Taiwan:
In Search of Identity

Thomas B. Gold

I n the early 1950's Taiwan seemed an unlikely candidate to become a model of economic or political development. It was overrun with refugees from the civil war on the Chinese mainland. Its economy was crippled by runaway inflation, its infrastructure and industrial plant bombed out. Defeated, bankrupt, and desperate, the ruling military regime was obsessed with returning to the mainland and treated the people of Taiwan with brutality. The island's immediate future looked bleak.

Barely thirty years later Taiwan was acclaimed as a miracle of economic growth. This growth, achieved concurrently with social equity and political stability, had brought the country close to developed nation status. In the late 1980's Taiwan attracted renewed attention as its longstanding authoritarian political system gave way to rapid democratization.

This chapter examines Taiwan's experience of economic development and political change. We look first at the period prior to the economic boom of the 1960's. Next comes an analysis of Taiwan's strategies for economic development and the roles of the three main actors—private capital, foreign corporations, and the state. The focus then shifts to Taiwan's political system and the dramatic breakthrough to democratization during the second half of the 1980's. Finally, we will consider some of the challenges Taiwan faces in the final decade of the twentieth century.

Four themes are woven through this discussion of Taiwan's recent history. One is the rapidity of change. In an extraordinarily short time, Taiwan was transformed from an agricultural country dependent on imports of manufactured

Thomas Gold teaches sociology and is Chair of the Center for Chinese Studies at the University of California, Berkeley. He has done extensive fieldwork on the Chinese mainland —where he was among the first American exchange scholars—and in Taiwan. He has written on a broad range of topics relating to socio-political change in these areas. His publications include *State and Society in the Taiwan Miracle* as well as more recent works on the development of the private sector in China.

Notes for this chapter can be found on pages 184–186

goods to one of the world's leading trading nations, specializing in increasingly sophisticated high-tech products. Its people moved from the countryside to the cities, rice paddies to corporate boardrooms, employment in agriculture to industry and services.

A second theme is Taiwan's linkage with the international system. The island has historically been part of larger entities. It has been a Chinese province and a Japanese colony. It has been an integral part of the United States-led anti-communist alliance. Taiwan's economy, culture, social structure, and political system have to varying degrees been shaped by its integration into global systems.

Third is Taiwan's dynamic readjustment to changing circumstances. Taiwan has aggressively positioned itself to carve out new niches in the world economy. Domestically, there has been constant readjustment in the relations between the party-state and society, a process which has gathered speed in recent years.

Finally, there is Taiwan's search for identity. Taiwan was settled from the seventeenth through the nineteenth centuries by Chinese imbued with Confucian, Buddhist, and Taoist traditions. Then, during fifty years as colonial occupiers, the Japanese tried to turn the Taiwanese into quasi-Japanese. When the island reverted to Chinese control in 1945, the Nationalists began to convert the citizenry back into Chinese, combining traditional values with the modern ideology of the National Father, Sun Yat-sen. But as a staunch American ally, Taiwan also received a constant influx of American values and popular culture. Since the 1970's many Taiwanese have begun to explore the nature of this cultural synthesis, seeking to define the essence of a Taiwanese identity and to determine how Taiwan should relate to the rest of the world, including mainland China.

Taiwan Before the Take-Off

"Taiwan" refers to one major island and several smaller islands which lie approximately 160 kilometers across the Taiwan Straits to the east of the Chinese mainland. The total area is slightly less than 36,000 square kilometers, making it about the same size as the Netherlands.

The spectacular mountain scenery of the main island is so striking that Portuguese sailors in the seventeenth century called it Ilha Formosa (beautiful island), a name still used today. The Chinese name, Tai-wan, also referring to the uneven topography, means "terraced bay."

Most of the population is concentrated in the large plain along the western coast, with other settlements scattered around the island. The population density in 1989 was more than 558 people per square kilometer. Taiwan has virtually no natural resources besides forests and moderate deposits of coal, natural gas, and some minerals.

The population of Taiwan exceeds twenty million. Some 300,000 inhabitants are so-called aborigines of Malayo-Polynesian origin who were driven from the plains into the mountains as other groups settled the island. Nearly all of the others are Han Chinese who have come from the mainland over the course of the last several hundred years. Manchu, Mongol, Tibetan, and Hui and other minority nationalities found in China are also represented on Taiwan.

The Chinese are further classified by when they or their ancestors came to Taiwan. Those who came prior to (or, in a few cases, during) the Japanese occupation from 1895 to 1945 are referred to as "Taiwanese." This group emigrated primarily from Quanzhou and Zhangzhou in the Minnan region of southern Fujian province; they speak a dialect called Hokkien, which is also common among other Chinese settler communities throughout Southeast Asia that trace their origins to Minnan. Other Taiwanese include immigrants from Guangdong province and the Hakkas, a Han group with a distinct language and culture that lives scattered throughout southern China.

On October 25, 1945, after Japan's defeat in World War II, Taiwan was returned to the Republic of China. Inhabitants of Taiwan who came to the island after this date are called "mainlanders." They hail from every province on the mainland, although a sizable proportion, including many top officials, came from the Yangtze River delta region around Shanghai.

The official language on Taiwan, the one taught in schools, is Mandarin or *kuo-yu* (national language). Based on the Peking dialect, it is the same as the official language on the mainland, where it is referred to as *putonghua* (common language). As on the mainland, many people in Taiwan speak native dialects among themselves, using Mandarin only for official functions or communication with people from other areas.

The original Han Chinese settlers brought the culture and social structure of the mainland with them to Taiwan. Central to this culture is Confucianism, the ethical system named after the fifth-century B.C. philosopher Confucius. Not exactly a religion, Confucianism is best conceived of as an ethic of social relations. Confucius lived at a time of great social upheaval, and he sought from that chaos to recreate a golden age of the past, the so-called Great Harmony (*datong*). His program stressed the Five Relationships: husband–wife, father–son, emperor–

minister, older brother–younger brother, and friend–friend. The first four are hierarchical, stratified by age or gender; Confucius argued that if all people performed their status roles within these relationships correctly, society would be harmonious. Chinese society was family based, and the emperor was like the father of the nation. If he and his ministers ruled well, society and nature would be peaceful and abundant. If the government was corrupt, there would be social unrest and natural disasters, indicating that the emperor had lost the Mandate of Heaven and could be overthrown. Chinese officials ruled by example rather than law.

Confucianism was clearly hierarchical and authoritarian. Its traditional value system ranked scholar-officials at the top, followed by farmers, artisans, and merchants. At the same time Confucianism had a democratic side. China invented a meritocratic civil service with qualifying examinations open to everyone. The famous Confucian saying "in education there is no class" meant that anyone was theoretically entitled to receive an education and take the tests. In practice, only wealthy Chinese could spare the labor of their sons (the democratic tendencies did not extend to sexual equality) and indulge them in the study of the Confucian classics that formed the core of the exams.

The Chinese believed strongly in diligence and frugality, however, and anyone could potentially accumulate the wealth to enter the upper class by another route. Although pre-modern China had a lively economy, merchants commonly did not invest their profits in expanding their enterprises. Rather, they used their money to buy official titles or to purchase land, thereby entering the higher-status landed gentry class. Then they set their sons to study to enter the bureaucracy through the front door.

Until the late nineteenth century Chinese officials on the mainland considered Taiwan a backwater. It was an undesirable posting. Prominent local families took over much of the responsibility for governing and maintaining social order. It took the threat of Western imperialism for the Manchu Qing (Ch'ing) dynasty to turn its attention seriously to the island. General Liu Ming-ch'uan arrived from the mainland to bolster the island's defenses, and in 1887 Taiwan was upgraded to provincial status.

Peking turned the island over to Japan after losing the Sino-Japanese War of 1894–95, however, and after weak resistance, Taiwan became the first colony of the last imperial power. Unlike the Chinese, the Japanese had responded to Western imperialism by studying the strengths of the invaders and adopting their techniques to regain autonomy and join the global power elite.

The Japanese learned that strong nations built empires, but Japanese imperialism differed in significant ways from that of the Western powers. The Japanese colonized Taiwan, Korea, and Manchuria, neighboring societies of people physically and culturally similar to themselves. These similarities reduced the culture clash typical of colonialism. Another difference was that the Japanese wanted to use Taiwan as a showcase to prove their equality with the white race; they set about aggressively investing in infrastructure, surveying the land, increasing agricultural productivity, establishing broad-based education, and introducing public health measures. The Japanese provided social mobility, mostly by offering the Taiwanese careers in medicine and teaching, although they treated them as inferiors. Finally, Japanese rule was seen as harsh but based on law. Certainly when compared to the chaos that engulfed mainland China during the same period, Taiwan was a model of stability and improving living standards. As the Japanese began to lose World War II and shipping to and from Taiwan was interrupted, they introduced some industry into Taiwan.

American bombing toward the end of the war reduced much of the island's industrial plant and infrastructure to rubble. Taiwan's situation deteriorated even further after the Japanese surrender. What had become a stable, productive society quickly reverted to lawlessness, chaos, and corruption as Taiwan became engulfed in the Chinese civil war.

Under the terms of the Cairo Declaration of 1943, Taiwan was handed back to China at the war's end. "China" was now the Republic of China (ROC), its capital Nanking. Under the leadership of Generalissimo Chiang Kai-shek and his Kuomintang (KMT or Nationalist) Party, China had struggled through eight years of brutal war against Japan and a simmering struggle against a communist rebellion. The communist insurgency heated up again in 1946, and once more China was plunged into instability, affecting the newly incorporated province of Taiwan.

Soon after Japan's surrender mainland carpetbaggers in and out of government came to plunder Taiwan, China's most developed province. The most egregious villain was the new governor, a Fujian warlord named Chen Yi. He was a man of unbridled corruption and arrogance, and in short order Taiwanese eager to transform themselves from colonials to citizens of the Republic became hostile and disillusioned. On February 28, 1947, after government agents beat a female black marketeer and shot a bystander (the "2.28 Incident"), Taiwanese anger exploded. Chiang Kai-shek sent troops to quell what expanded into an island-wide rebellion. Estimates of the death toll range upwards of 20,000 victims, including a significant proportion of the intellectual and social elite.

The KMT labelled the movement a communist rebellion. It was not, although some communist agents participated. The insensitivity of the mainland government to the devastation of the island and the brutality of the crackdown created a profound rift between mainlanders and Taiwanese. The islanders became leaderless, quiescent, and apolitical. They had learned a horrible lesson.

Meanwhile the KMT, despite huge American backing, lost its war against the Communists' peasant armies, and began evacuating troops, civilians, and assets to Taiwan. The island's population rose from about 6 million in 1945 to 8 million in 1951. Corruption, inflation, and disorder accompanied this expansion. The American government gave up on Chiang Kai-shek, planning to wait until the dust settled and then make amends with the Chinese Communists. Chiang prepared to move to Taiwan to make a last stand. He sent his son Ching-kuo to stabilize the island politically, and Ching-kuo pursued his task ruthlessly, setting up an elaborate internal security apparatus that penetrated the party, the army, the state, and society at large. The regime declared martial law in December 1949, tightening its grip in preparation for Armageddon, but the final battle never came. Instead the North Korean invasion of South Korea on June 25, 1950, prompted a renewed American commitment to Chiang Kai-shek and a determination to stop communism in Asia.

For his part, Chiang initiated a two-year purge and reform of the KMT in an effort to create an organization capable of withstanding a communist invasion and, eventually, of governing all of China. The Americans provided military and civilian assistance. They also sent advisors who acted as something of a shadow government, counseling the KMT and using American control of funding and raw materials to induce the Chinese to accept their advice. Humiliated by defeat, surrounded by a hostile population, and bankrupt, the KMT had little choice.

Chiang's regime, now stranded on the island, adopted new tactics to deal with the Taiwanese. With American urging, it undertook a land reform. Chiang's reliance on the political support of land-owning elites in China had prevented his ever trying such reform on the mainland despite its central place in the official ideology; but as an occupying power without a local base in Taiwan, he could afford to expropriate land from Taiwanese landlords. The redistribution of land was effected without violence by compulsorily purchasing land above a fixed acreage and selling it to the tillers. This reform left small landowning families as the dominant force in the countryside and established a foundation for relatively equitable income distribution.

Through the Joint Sino-American Commission on Rural Reconstruction, the government went on to organize peasants into credit and marketing cooperatives and to provide new technology. Taiwan's support of agriculture and its delay in industrialization stand in sharp contrast to virtually every other developing country in the postwar world. Taiwan did squeeze agriculture somewhat, however, in order to feed the cities and supply industry by compelling peasants to trade rice at a low price for high-priced, state-monopolized chemical fertilizer.

By 1952 Taiwan's economy had recovered to prewar peaks and the political situation had stabilized. American advisors from the State Department's International Cooperation Administration (ICA) [later to become the Agency for International Development (AID)] sat in on many Chinese government agency meetings concerning economic policy. Much of the policy implementation fell to the Council on U.S. Aid (CUSA), an extra-ministerial body comprising cabinet ministers and chaired by the premier. CUSA enjoyed substantial autonomy from political interference as it worked to dispense American aid of food, clothing, and military assistance. American aid accounted for approximately 40% of capital formation in Taiwan during the 1950's.

Economic policy in the 1950's stressed Import Substituting Industrialization (ISI)—that is, the substitution of domestic production for imports in order to conserve scarce foreign exchange and to build an indigenous industrial base. The government erected tariff barriers against imports to shelter these infant industries and provided other forms of assistance such as low-interest loans to selected industries. An overvalued currency discouraged exports, but facilitated the importation of capital goods necessary for production.

The government selected a small group of businessmen to spearhead ISI, mostly capitalists who had followed Chiang Kai-shek from the mainland. They included Shanghainese in the cotton textile industry and Shandongese in flour milling and textiles. By monopolizing the production of necessities, these men initially earned windfall profits, though by the end of the decade they had saturated the market and were engaging in price slashing tactics to survive. Nevertheless, ISI succeeded in stimulating domestic industry and thus attracting the attention of many other potential local investors. Energy, talent, and capital were accumulating, but the macro business climate required fundamental reforms in order to open the field to more than a handful of state-supported players.

With American assistance Chiang Kai-shek had stabilized Taiwan, but he still saw the island's development primarily in terms of building a base to reconquer the mainland. It was not until the 1960's that the ROC government shifted its focus to the development of the island for its own benefit.

The Economy Takes Off

From the mid-1960's onward Taiwan's economy grew with extraordinary swiftness. The structural changes that accompanied the industrial revolutions in Europe and America took 150 years to complete; Taiwan's transformation took only forty years. The rapidity of the changes can be seen in GNP growth rates, which averaged 7.5% annually from 1953 to 1962, 10.8% from 1963 to 1972, and 8.4% from 1973 to 1988. Even in the relatively slow year of 1989, GNP grew by over 7%. Per capita GNP grew from US$ 50 in 1952 to $161 in 1961 and approximately $7,500 in 1989.

The statistics on structural changes also reflect this rapid growth. The contribution of agriculture to Net Domestic Product (NDP) fell from 36% in 1952 to 29.4% in 1962, 18.9% in 1969, 9.2% in 1980, and just below 6% in 1989. Industry's share, by contrast, rose from 18% in 1952 to 30.8% in 1967, 40.3% in 1972, and a high of 47% in 1986 and 1987. The proportion of manufacturing also increased dramatically, from 10.8% of NDP in 1952 to 39.4% in 1987. The service sector's contribution to NDP remained relatively constant, hovering at 46% to 47% over the same period. Since the 1950's Taiwan's foreign debt has been low and manageable, running at a very small percentage of exports.

The shifting composition of exports also illustrates rapid structural change. In 1952 agricultural products contributed 22.1% of export value, processed agricultural products 69.8%, and industrial products only 8.1%. By 1989 processed and unprocessed agricultural products accounted for less than 5% of export value, with industrial products making up the remainder. The composition of industrial exports has also changed dramatically. For much of the postwar period, textile products led the export growth. In 1984 electrical machinery and apparatus overtook textiles, and the gap continued to widen until in 1988 it approached two to one: exported electrical goods were valued at at US$ 16.6 billion, textile exports at US$ 8.9 billion. Metal manufactures, machinery, plastic articles, and chemicals were other leading export items.

The major reason for the speedy growth of Taiwan's economy was the extraordinary expansion of exports, which grew at an average annual rate of 19.5% from 1953 to 1962, 29.9% from 1963 to 1972, and 18.2% from 1973 to 1988. In 1952 foreign trade accounted for 23% of GNP; exports accounted for 8.5%. In 1973, on the eve of the first oil crisis, the figures were 77% and 41.6% respectively. Preliminary figures for 1989 are 78.8% and 44%. Per capita value of trade reached US$ 5,923 in 1989, $3,310 of which was exports. This was no accident, but the result of a deliberate and fundamental shift in government policies away from the highly protectionist anti-export ISI policies of the 1950's to the export-oriented strategy that has dominated government planning ever since.

We now tend to think of Taiwan as a highly focused export machine, but its transition to an export orientation was by no means inevitable. The government's financial weakness, its desire to maintain control over the economy, and its overriding concern for survival made it hesitant to surrender Taiwan's economy to the vagaries of the global economy. There was a question about which industries could lead the export charge. The inefficiency of Taiwan's highly protected light industries made them unlikely candidates for success in the international market-place. Developing new industries would require heavy capital investment—and the capital wasn't there. Many politicians were reluctant to invite foreign investment to finance internationalization, fearing a revival of the days on the mainland when foreigners enjoyed special privileges and immunity from Chinese law under a system called extraterritoriality.

The decision to change Taiwan's economic orientation so fundamentally was due in no small part to American pressure. ICA/AID, which had initially concentrated on rehabilitating and stabilizing the island's economy, redefined its mission for Taiwan as economic development, and in 1960 announced that it would begin phasing out its Taiwan program altogether since the island was ready to "graduate" and go it alone. Analysts concluded that exports of manufactured goods and an infusion of foreign capital could best stimulate the economy. To this end, Chinese and American officials designed a package of reforms to lower some tariffs, reduce the number of goods which could not be imported, promote and subsidize exports, and stimulate local and foreign private investment. One difficult reform was eliminating multiple exchange rates for the New Taiwan Dollar and settling on a uniform rate; the exchange rate held steady at NT$ 40 to US$ 1 for more than fifteen years. The government held on to many of the instruments it used to control the economy, such as protective tariffs, export subsidies, state enterprises, and bank ownership. But it dismantled enough of the 1950's ISI system to enable exports and foreign investment to expand rapidly.

The timing of these reforms was fortuitous. In the mid-1960's world trade expanded with the relaxation of cold war tensions, although the Vietnam War greatly stimulated trade and industrialization in East Asia. Japan in particular took advantage of this expansion, flooding the American market with low-cost textiles, plastics, and electronic products. In order to remain competitive in their own market, American manufacturers went offshore in search of production locations where costs were lower than at home. It was at exactly this juncture that Taiwan began aggressively to solicit foreign investment and AID helped to publicize the island as a suitable place for potential investors. One of Taiwan's strongest selling points was a labor force that was cheap, disciplined, efficient, and well educated.

As American firms began to recapture market share, their Japanese competitors were forced to seek cheaper offshore production sites, bringing them to Taiwan as well. Thus the search by multinationals to remain competitive in the global marketplace, combined with Taiwan's aggressive solicitation, brought increasing numbers of foreign investors to the island.

Among the island's advantages was the Kaohsiung Export Processing Zone in southern Taiwan. Opened in 1966, it was the first facility of its kind anywhere, combining a modern harbor, an industrial park, and a centralized administration that could make decisions quickly without bureaucratic red tape. Investors—local or foreign—could import equipment and raw materials duty free as long as they exported everything they produced; they also enjoyed other incentives such as tax holidays. The Zone offered an abundant, cheap labor force, since it attracted thousands of young girls from nearby farms who planned to work for a few years, sending money home and accumulating enough for their dowries. Initially this cheap labor was the Zone's primary attraction for foreign firms.

At first these firms imported all the parts they needed; Taiwan could produce neither the type nor quality of components they required. But aggressive matchmaking by the government introduced foreign investors to local manufacturers eager to learn how to produce new goods that met international standards. Local suppliers could, and did, cut costs even further, and the value added in Taiwan soon expanded from simple assembly labor to the production of a large proportion of the parts for the exported items. This development served at the same time to transfer technology to Taiwan, as the Zone evolved from an enclave into a production center with multiple linkages throughout the national economy.

External markets supplanted the small domestic market as the source of economic dynamism. The Zone was by no means the only source of exports. More and more local businesses took up the challenge offered by the international market; however, lacking knowledge of foreign markets and tastes and the resources to conduct market research and brand name development, the majority relied on subcontracting and consignment production for foreign companies in order to export. A mass buyer like Sears or K-Mart would visit Taiwanese factories and order goods in bulk for sale under the chain's brand name. A company like Arrow Shirts or U.S. Shoe would supply samples to several factories, selecting one or more on the basis of quality and cost to produce to specifications, again under the foreign brand name. The latter method, called Original Equipment Manufacture (OEM), stimulated the fantastic growth of Taiwan's consumer electronics industry. Local manufacturers learned how and what to produce for the international market. The "Made in Taiwan" label spread worldwide, even if no one outside Taiwan knew a single Taiwanese brand name. Thousands of tiny trading companies sprang up to link foreign buyers and local producers or to export directly, creating a trading structure quite different from that of the huge trading firms in Japan and South Korea.

The oil crises of 1974 and 1980 played havoc with Taiwan's oil-dependent and export-oriented economy. Production costs rose just as global recession settled in. In the second half of the 1970's, the government took steps to restructure Taiwan's economy so that the country could better withstand circumstances beyond its control. The state committed massive amounts of planning and capital with its US$ 8 billion Ten Major Development Projects. These projects included the first major investment in infrastructure since the Japanese occupation: the North-South Expressway, the Chiang Kai-shek International Airport, harbor development, railroad electrification, nuclear power plants, the East Coast railway, and additional export processing zones. Others of these development projects—in shipbuilding, integrated steel milling, petrochemical complexes—were production oriented.

The petrochemical plants had been on the books prior to the oil crisis as a means to integrate vertically two of Taiwan's most important industries, synthetic fibers and plastics. But they were extraordinarily costly and polluting. After the first oil crisis the government decided to forego future development of heavy industry and concentrate instead on technology-intensive, high-value-added sectors like computers, robotics, biotechnology, and telecommunications. Taiwan decided to follow the Japanese example and let labor-intensive, low-value-added sunset sectors, such as parts of the textile and footware industries, die out or migrate abroad.

In addition to offering special incentives to investors in targeted industries, in 1980 the government created a new industrial zone, the Science Based Industrial Park in Hsin-chu, 110 kilometers outside Taipei. The Park was designed to look like Silicon Valley in the hope of luring back to Taiwan many Chinese who had gone abroad to study and never returned and of attracting other foreign and overseas Chinese investors. Located near two first-rate universities with strong engineering and science programs and the state-run Industrial Technology and Research Institute, the Park supports Taiwanese research and development, upgrading the island's industrial structure.

Taiwan's ability to read and respond quickly to international signals has relied on the private sector and on the central role of the state. Taiwan's private sector has grown and evolved quickly. Japanese corporations dominated Taiwan's economy during the colonial period. After the island returned to Chinese control in 1945, a handful of capitalists from the mainland, relying on state support, emerged as the first captains of industry. They dominated the textile and flour milling industries and then diversified as a wide range of new industries took root on the island.

At the same time numerous Taiwanese of all backgrounds began to invest in small-scale enterprises in commerce, services, and industry. A few received AID

Taiwan

September 28, Confucius' birthday, is also Teachers' Day. The *pa-yi* dance is performed by juvenile dancers at every Confucian temple as a mark of respect for the great teacher.

The Yushan (Jade Mountain) is a majestic highlight of Taiwan's national park system.

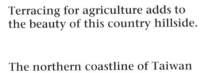

Terracing for agriculture adds to the beauty of this country hillside.

The northern coastline of Taiwan (far left) is noted for its many scenic rock formations and its white sand beaches.

Face masks partially screen the smoke-polluted air from heavy industry in Kao-Hsuing as commuters ride motorbikes to and from work.

Elaborate traditional costumes characterize the celebration of Taiwan's many religious festivals and holidays.

Young Taiwanese enjoy the elegance of a wine house in Taipei.

Elderly members of Taiwan's Legislative Yuan are relaxing.

Generalissimo Chiang Kai-Shek at his residence in Chungking, in quieter days before military defeats forced him, in December, 1949, to leave the mainland for Taiwan.

Tea, one of Taiwan's exports for centuries, is grown today in this Alishan high-hill tea garden.

A street scene at night in Taipei.

The high standard of living in Taiwan permits nearly all families to purchase what they need in shops or markets.

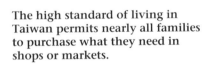

Primary school children at play.

Nearly all of Taiwan's school-age children attend elementary school, and almost half go to college.

The low wall of Lungshan Temple is a good place for the elderly to meet with friends on a sunny day.

Training in science and technology is emphasized by the Taiwanese so that economic development may be sustained.

These young women require magnifying equipment to assemble micro integrated circuits.

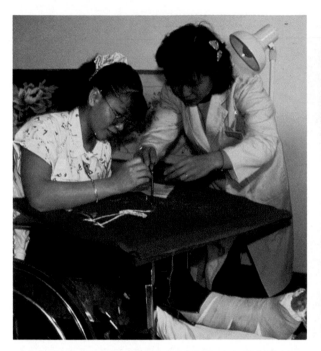

Agricultural technology is applied toward the improvement of both the quality and the productivity of the tea crop.

The handicapped receive therapy (upper left) and vocational training, and have been provided increased easy access to public facilities.

The 519 Incident: demonstration at the Chiang Kai-Shek Memorial, May, 1986.

Robotic equipment does the soldering in this automotive assembly plant.

The Republic of China's heavy industry is dependent on the products of the China Steel Corporation and the China Shipbuilding Corporation.

A cornfield worker (far left) in Tainan, the breadbasket of Taiwan.

Taiwan's many chemical and petrochemical plants provide products that have supported its industrial growth, but also with unwanted air pollution.

The 1989 Nationality Day (Double Tenth) celebration in Presidential Square. Double Tenth (October 10, thus 10-10) celebrates the beginning in 1911 of the overthrow of the Manchu Qing Dynasty, making possible the founding of the Republic of China.

President Lee waving to the crowd in the Double Tenth celebration shown above.

Exhibits of export goods at a trade fair in Taiwan's World Trade Center attract buyers from countries throughout the world.

These Red Cross workers are accepting applications from Taiwanese for visits to relatives in previously prohibited mainland China.

This container ship, carrying a full load of the island's products, is part of the tremendous export capability of Taiwan.

Taipei's Grand Hotel combines modern luxury with architecture in a traditional Chinese style.

The picture at left shows a main business street in Taipei in 1949.

A current photograph shows the transformation that has taken place in the city.

support; with such support Wang Yung-ch'ing in plastics and Lin T'ing-sheng in electronics, for example, built two of Taiwan's largest conglomerates, the Formosa Plastics and Tatung groups. But most entrepreneurs had to rely solely on their own savings and on loans from relatives and friends in order to start up small businesses. These were nearly all family enterprises in which all members of the family worked in the business and nearly all employees were family members.

Mainlanders monopolized the political system as well as the economic high ground, putting these areas largely beyond the reach of ordinary Taiwanese. In any case, after the bloody 2.28 Incident in 1947 Taiwanese wanted to avoid dealing with the mainlander regime as much as possible. A division of labor evolved, with mainlanders dominating the party, the state, and the military, and Taiwanese increasingly running private business.

For its part the government did not much interfere in small-scale entrepreneur-ship, and as it became more stable and self-assured, the regime worked hard to improve the business climate for all investors. The obvious success of many businessmen had a demonstration effect on their neighbors, and Taiwan's private sector exploded. Taiwan still pulses with the nearly anarchic energy of family-based entrepreneurs starting up new ventures and scouting out opportunities with astounding speed and flexibility. Taiwanese businessmen rode the wave of the 1960's economic boom. Many benefited through contacts with foreign investors, serving as suppliers, subcontractors, and even joint venture partners. Taiwanese dominated consumer electronics and also moved decisively into textiles, machin-ery, and virtually every other industrial sector.

Most of the founding entrepreneurs were poorly educated, but they invested in advanced education for their children. With foreign MBA's their sons and daughters helped to build diversified conglomerates. The history of the Shin Kong group illustrates this process. Its founder, Ho-su Wu, got his start under the Japanese as an apprentice in a Japanese cloth shop, then opened his own store, trading first with Japan and then with mainland China. During the land reform period after 1945, he purchased a woolen mill. With state and AID assistance Wu later opened Taiwan's first manmade fiber factory. The elder Wu had little formal education, but he sent his children to study for advanced degrees in the United States and Japan. They now run the group, which in addition to textiles includes department stores, gas, life insurance, real estate, and securities companies. Many other entrepreneurs followed a similar path; in this way Taiwan has developed large business groups which are still family based and which form complex networks with other groups. But the vast majority of Taiwanese businesses remain very small. In 1986, 91.2% of manufacturing enterprises had fewer than fifty workers; 34.5% of workers in manufacturing establishments were in enterprises with fewer than fifty workers.

Quite naturally the rise of a capitalist class in Taiwan was accompanied by the emergence of an industrial working class. Taiwan's proletariat has avoided antagonistic relations with capitalists and has never developed a labor movement. One reason is that many employees in the tiny enterprises that dominate the private sector are family members. The work force in many other industries is comprised of young girls who think of themselves not as lifelong workers, but as temporary employees supporting rural families and saving for their dowries. Taiwan's rural population earns approximately three-fourths of its income from such non-agricultural activities as working for wages and running small businesses. Here, too, there is no full-time proletariat.

Many blue-collar workers do not view themselves as permanent members of the working class. They work for someone else only long enough to accumulate capital to start their own businesses, in some cases hoping to become suppliers or subcontractors to their former employers. So a number of social and economic factors have militated against the formation of a working-class consciousness in Taiwan. Political considerations have also had an effect: martial law regulations made strikes a capital offense until 1987, and the KMT controls the labor unions.

Foreign investors have played a vital role in Taiwan's economic development, but their contribution has been channeled into a limited number of sectors, and the net effects through forward and backward linkages outweigh the absolute investment figures. Taiwan's own savings rate is exceptionally high (over 30% of GNP for most of the past two decades), and foreign investment as a percentage of Gross Domestic Capital Formation has been quite low in the aggregate (slightly over 6% in 1987).

Much of foreign investors' activity has been focused on consignment buying and subcontracting. American multinational firms, which account for about one-third of total foreign capital, have typically set up wholly-owned subsidiaries in Taiwan and targeted the American market. By the 1970's, for example, virtually every American brand name in the television industry had an assembly operation in Taiwan. Japanese investors, who account for about one-fourth of foreign investment, commonly adopted a different strategy. They took local partners and aimed for Taiwan's domestic market and for exports to anywhere but Japan. The Taiwanese partner would often hold the majority of shares, but the management was Japanese. Agreements compelled the importation of Japanese parts. Many medium-sized Japanese firms followed their Japanese customers to Taiwan. Most of the foreign technology that came to the island in this way was labor intensive and obsolete back home, but still advanced for Taiwan. Taiwanese partners and suppliers quickly adopted this technology, spreading it and thereby upgrading the island's productive capacity.

The state, however, has been the major player in Taiwan's economy. Government agencies own enterprises at several levels. The most powerful include China Petroleum (which monopolizes oil imports), Taiwan Power, China Steel, BES Engineering (which has developed much of the infrastructure in Taiwan and has an extensive international clientele), Taiwan Fertilizer, and Taiwan Tobacco and Wine Monopoly. Not only are these corporations large in themselves, most ranking among the largest 100 companies in Taiwan, but they control vital inputs for the downstream private sector. The large synthetic textile and plastics industries, for example, are all in one way or another dependent on the government for their raw materials. To be sure, Taiwan's private sector has grown faster than the public sector, and asset ownership is overwhelmingly (over 80%) in private hands. But state enterprises occupy a strategic position in Taiwan. The KMT also owns several companies in a range of sectors, especially the media, entertainment, and finance.

Apart from state-owned enterprises, the government has invested billions of dollars in physical infrastructure. Since the 1970's it has undertaken dozens of major projects. It has also invested heavily in the cultivation of human capital through the education system and, more recently, through research and development.

The government exerts economic influence though a number of other means. It owns at least 50% of all banks, giving it enormous control over the private sector's access to capital. The government publishes market-oriented and indicative economic plans. It selects industries for special encouragement, offering incentives and protection for targeted sectors. The government collects and disseminates reams of data on the global economy which it makes available to all interested parties. Finally, the government helps the private sector negotiate with foreign trading partners and investors. It tries to deflect foreign anger and protectionist sentiments. It has organized regular "Buy America Missions," bringing Taiwanese businessmen to the United States to sign high-profile deals and publicize Taiwan's sincere desire to redress the multi-billion-dollar trade deficit between the two partners.

Why has the state played such a large role in Taiwan's capitalist economy? One reason is ideological: in his writings the National Father, Sun Yat-sen, advocated that the state own industries vital to defense or national survival and industries whose capital requirements exceed the resources of the private sector. He also favored government restriction of the private sector to prevent the social inequality that arises from the concentration of too much wealth in private hands. The policy of restricting private capital has helped Taiwan achieve an excellent record on equitable income distribution. It has also prevented the growth of conglomerates on the scale of Japan's *zaibatsu* or South Korea's *chaebol*.

But the state's dominant role also derives from Taiwan's history. Chiang Kai-shek's emigre regime saw itself as a temporary force occupying one small province of the country. Chiang needed to marshal resources for a return to the mainland, and controlling the economy was a means to fund his gargantuan war machine, regulate the private sector, and dispense strategic favors to supporters. Interventionist government policy prevented the Taiwanese from controlling enough wealth to pose a challenge to the mainlanders' dominance.

Economic development in Taiwan has been fundamentally a political process. Because the KMT regime came from outside the island and established its dominance over the Taiwanese through brute force, it has used economic development as the basis for its claim to legitimacy. With American backing Chiang Kai-shek favored economic pragmatists over ideologues in the 1950's, promoting a cohort of talented mainlanders to guide development. These men were foreign-trained technocrats, most of whom were trained as engineers, not as economists. K. Y. Yin, K. T. Li, and Y. S. Sun, among others, formulated and implemented bold policies through planning agencies which enjoyed a great deal of autonomy from political pressure. American consulting companies such as J. G. White Engineering, Stanford Research Institute, and Arthur D. Little were hired to assist in project evaluation and strategic planning. The state has continually had to maintain the investment climate and find ways to keep the economy growing to buy off popular discontent. The KMT can also hold up Taiwan's economic success as a challenge to the communists on the mainland, demonstrating that the island represents an alternative and superior Chinese system.

Several factors have contributed to the state's success in implementing its economic policies. The government's emigre status and lack of Taiwanese roots kept it immune from social pressures, an enormous advantage that allowed the state to press forward with policies such as land reform, export orientation, preferential treatment of selected sectors, and foreign investment, any of which might have generated opposition from powerful entrenched interests in other societies. Also crucial was the growing perception that the state was really committed to Taiwan's development and that its policies were well informed, well intentioned, and thus deserving of support. The control of corruption after the 1950–52 purge and the demonstrated subsequent success of private business granted legitimacy to the state and its economic role. On the other side of the equation, the state's control of resources gave it a powerful material base from which to implement policy and ensure compliance.

Over time the state's economic dominance has waned somewhat, and the role of the vital Taiwanese-dominated private sector has expanded dramatically. But it would be a serious error to underestimate the role of the state in creating and guiding Taiwan's economic miracle.

The Political System Catches Up

Taiwan was exceptional in undergoing such a revolutionary transformation of its economic and social systems while maintaining a political system seemingly impervious to change. Yet the political monolith began to give way at the end of the 1980's.

There is no country called Taiwan. The KMT-led government of the ROC claims that it was driven off the Chinese mainland in 1949 by the Communists to its temporary home in Taiwan province with its temporary capital in Taipei. It claims a historic mission to recover the mainland from the Communists. For their part the Communists insist that Taiwan is a province of the People's Republic of China (PRC); their historic mission is to reunify the motherland under their leadership.

Neither the Taipei-based Nationalists nor the Beijing-based Communists permit dual recognition of both regimes. Other nations thus must choose one or the other as representing all of China. Until the early 1970's, as a legacy of the Cold War, most chose Taipei. President Richard Nixon's visit to the mainland in 1972 lent irresistible momentum to an international movement to change policy, however. On January 1, 1979, the United States recognized the PRC as the sole government of all China, thereby de-recognizing the ROC. As of late 1990, only about two dozen countries continue to maintain diplomatic relations with Taipei, and several of those, including South Korea, have put Taipei on notice that they are seeking formal relations with Beijing. Nevertheless, virtually every nation in the world maintains economic ties with Taiwan, and in several cases both sides have opened trade offices which function as quasi-consulates.

When the KMT government moved to Taiwan province, it brought along in addition to a huge military force its organs of state. Chief among the appointed bodies is the Executive Yuan, or cabinet, whose president is also the premier. The elected bodies include the Legislative Yuan, which passes legislation and approves the budget; the Control Yuan, derived from China's traditional censorate, a watchdog agency; and the National Assembly, which elects the president and vice-president and amends the constitution.

Under provisions of the 1947 constitution, elections were held in 1947 for each of the three elected bodies, but the worsening civil war prompted a series of special stipulations which circumvented the constitution and in effect froze the political system for decades. The Provisional Amendments for the Period of Mobilization of the Suppression of Communist Rebellion ("Temporary Provisions"), promulgated on May 10, 1948, and amended at intervals thereafter, granted extraordinary powers to the president and permitted an extension of his tenure and that of the vice-president beyond the two-term limit. They also permitted members of the three national representative bodies who had earlier been elected on the mainland to keep their seats until new elections can be held for all China, effectively granting them lifetime tenure. Under the Temporary Provisions, the Executive Yuan declared martial law in December 1949. In 1967 President Chiang established a National Security Council composed of top civilian and military leaders to make key policy decisions. The Executive Yuan and the National Security Council have played a central role in maintaining Taiwan's political system.

The area of jurisdiction of the ROC government is in effect coextensive with that of the Taiwan Provincial Government. The members of the Taiwan Provincial Assembly have been directly elected since 1954. Taiwan also has directly elected county and municipal assemblies and officials.

Understanding the formal structure of government provides only a partial glimpse of the workings of Taiwan's political system. To grasp the whole we need to look at the Kuomintang Party.

The KMT was founded at the turn of the century by Sun Yat-sen, a doctor turned revolutionary. With the fledgling Chinese Communist Party, with which it had formed an alliance, the KMT underwent restructuring in 1923–24 by agents of the Comintern who rebuilt it along the lines of the Communist Party of the Soviet Union as established by V. I. Lenin.

The KMT has a National Congress, Central Committee, and Central Standing Committee, the last being the locus of real power. The KMT retains its Leninist essence: it conceives of itself as a vanguard party, admitting only the most advanced elements in society committed to achieving the party's historic mission; it is organized hierarchically along democratic-centralist principles; and it establishes cells throughout the government, military, and society. Until the democratic breakthrough in 1989, the party designated only one KMT-led organization to serve as the official societal organ for specific groups such as farmers, workers, and students. No independent competing social organizations, including political parties, were permitted.

For most of the KMT's history the lines between the party and the state have been blurred, hence the term "party-state." Chiang Kai-shek, Chiang Ching-kuo, and Lee Teng-hui all concurrently served as chairman of the KMT and president of the ROC. The party controlled appointments to the state bureaucracy. It formulated major policies for discussion and approval by the Executive Yuan. Its members dominated the elected bodies as well, and were obliged to follow party discipline, vote as instructed, and not embarrass government officials during questioning. Political commissars in the military ensured the armed forces' loyalty to the party. The KMT dominated the media and maintained a heavy ideological component in the educational system. The national anthem was the party anthem.

The KMT is not a *Marxist*-Leninist party, however, in that it does not conceive of itself as representing the interests of a particular class, and hence avoids class struggle; it reserves an important permanent role for private capital and does not intend to eliminate the market; and it does not intend to build communism. Rather the KMT regards constitutional democracy as an ideal form of government, the third and final stage in a sequence that began with military rule and was followed by tutelary rule by the KMT. The third stage began with the 1947 constitution, only to be suspended soon after. The KMT's ideology is the so-called Three Principles of the People: nationalism, democracy, and people's livelihood, the last comprising a number of socialist elements.

To his credit, Chiang Kai-shek drew a lesson from his crushing humiliation on the mainland. He undertook a purge to cleanse and rededicate the KMT. The members who came to Taiwan were united and cohesive, more easily managed than the factions on the mainland, and they had a much smaller territory and population to govern. They had learned a lesson. They brooked no dissent. The United States provided generous assistance, including its support of the ROC's occupation of "the China seat" in international organizations, without compelling the regime to liberalize.

For decades social scientists have debated about the relationship between economic, social, and political change. In the 1950's many theorists optimistically predicted that economic modernization in the Third World would bring about a more differentiated, complex social structure, one that would include an affluent and educated middle class. The new middle class, according to this model, would demand autonomy to make decisions regarding business and professional affairs, thereby compelling political democratization. In other words, capitalism and democracy went hand in hand and were mutually reinforcing.

Taiwan's experience pointed to a very different outcome: authoritarianism appeared if anything to be more conducive to development, and the middle classes apparently preferred the stability of dictatorship to the uncertainties of democracy. Taiwan's rapid economic development and social structural change, including the growth of a middle class, under stable authoritarian rule, baffled many theorists.

During the 1950's something of a liberal forum developed around a group of intellectuals of mainland origin connected with the journal *Free China Fortnightly*. The regime shut them down in 1960, however, when they tried to form a political party. Later generations of political reformers viewed the arrested leader of this group, Lei Chen, as a martyr.

Changes in the ROC's political fortunes abroad had domestic repercussions in the early 1970's. In 1971 the United States decided to return to Japan a group of islands which the ROC also claimed. Taiwanese students all over the world broke their long silence to protest both the American decision and their government's weak response. Also in 1971 the ROC's stalwart ally Richard Nixon stunned the world by announcing his plan to visit the Chinese mainland and to normalize relations with the PRC, and the United Nations voted to give the China seat to Beijing, forcing a withdrawal by the ROC delegation.

The mood in Taiwan turned sharply pessimistic. This series of humiliations and the government's demonstrated impotence galvanized some members of the middle class to act. Students and some young intellectuals, mostly Taiwanese, began to question KMT rule and the nature of Taiwanese society in a new journal, *The Intellectual (Daxue)*. They lacked a coherent strategy, were co-opted by the KMT, and failed to build a mass movement, but they had attracted attention. By the end of the decade they formed a core of opposition.

Chiang Ching-kuo became premier in 1972 as his father's health deteriorated. Ching-kuo had earned a reputation for intolerance of dissent, yet he immediately initiated processes that raised pressures for democratization.

First he began to recruit more Taiwanese into prominent positions in the party and state at the national level. Taiwanese already made up something like 70% of the membership of the KMT, and they held dominant positions in provincial and local politics. Chiang Kai-shek had selected a Taiwanese vice-president. To a certain extent Chiang Ching-kuo was accepting the reality that the children of mainlanders who went abroad rarely returned; someone had to fill the vacancies. Over the previous two decades Taiwanese had received the same education as the mainlanders' children, and the two groups increasingly shared a common culture. Although the Taiwanese were eminently qualified for top positions, however, political sensitivities and suspicions about their genuine loyalty to the mission of recovering the mainland prevented their being promoted until Chiang Ching-kuo took the initiative.

Lee Teng-hui is an example of this new generation of politically influential Taiwanese. A Cornell Ph.D. and agricultural economist, he was appointed by Chiang as mayor of Taipei, governor of Taiwan, and a member of the KMT's Central Standing Committee. Another prominent Taiwanese politician is Lin Yang-kang, who preceded Lee in the same appointed posts and has also served as vice premier and president of the Judicial Yuan. Lin also built an electoral base and mounted a brief challenge to Lee's campaign for the presidency in 1990. Kao Yu-jen, speaker of Taiwan's provincial assembly in the 1980's, is another Taiwanese political figure who rose to prominence under Chiang.

In addition to promoting Taiwanese, Chiang Ching-kuo built a technocracy. Highly educated officials replaced ideologues. The party and state concentrated on solving technical problems such as improving the investment climate and upgrading the industrial structure. Most of these new technocrats had pursued postgraduate studies abroad and had a more cosmopolitan view than their predecessors. As the ROC lost its international identity, and economic relations began to replace formal diplomatic relations, a new breed of leaders was ready to manage these linkages.

Chiang also recruited younger people of all provincial origins into top echelons. One high flyer is Ma Ying-jeou, a lawyer trained at New York University and Harvard. Ma was deputy secretary general of the KMT before his fortieth birthday. Some of these young officials, like Chen Li-an, Frederick Chien, and James Soong are the offspring of mainland elites. Inevitably, the members of this new generation have less sense of greater China than their parents, regardless of provincial origin. They have focused their primary energies onto the immediate task of developing Taiwan.

The 1970's in Taiwan saw the growth of a middle class. Many Taiwanese, having studied or traveled abroad, were positioned in the private business sector, universities, think tanks, and government units. Increasingly affluent, educated, and sophisticated, the members of this new social stratum began to take control over more aspects of their lives. Influenced by decades of bombardment on the one hand by American popular culture and values, and on the other by the regime's claim to be "Free China," they began to ask questions about the nature of Taiwan's increasingly complex society. A group of literary figures reflected this questioning, shifting the focus of their work away from greater China to the common people of Taiwan.

Elements of this middle class began to coalesce in a political movement in the late 1970's. Many were ex-KMT members frustrated with the party gerontocracy's obstinacy. In September 1977 they supported the independent campaign of Hsu Hsin-liang (a former rising star of the KMT expelled from the party for breach of discipline) for the magistracy of T'ao-yuan county. The KMT engaged in underhanded tactics to undermine Hsu, only increasing his popularity. On election night a riot broke out in the town of Chung-li in protest against KMT ballot tampering. It was the first such outbreak of spontaneous violence since the 2.28 Incident three decades earlier. The KMT backed down and Hsu took office, although he was hounded out a few years later.

The movement grew, styling itself the *dangwai* or "outside the party," the party referred to, of course, being the KMT. The KMT adamantly refused to allow the establishment of a new party, pointing to the Temporary Provisions and the fear that a multi-party system would open the door to instability. *Dangwai* members began to coordinate campaigns for the national elections scheduled for December 1978.

The elections were cancelled, however, when the United States suddenly announced its intention to establish diplomatic relations with Beijing, thereby dropping Taipei.

Some *dangwai* activists took this as a sign of KMT vulnerability and pushed even harder for political reform, and especially for the establishment of a new party. Centered around a new magazine called *Formosa,* members opened regional offices around the island. They held a mass rally in Kaohsiung on December 10, 1979, International Human Rights Day. The rally ended in a riot which many observers argued was instigated by police agents. The government put virtually the entire *dangwai* leadership on trial, sentencing them to long jail terms. *Dangwai* members who had not been charged and the wives of jailed activists scored decisive electoral victories when the postponed elections were held in 1980.

Under a more moderate leadership and with support from overseas Taiwanese and others interested in pressing for democratization (particularly Americans), the *dangwai* movement continued to grow. The proportion of new members of the national elective bodies elected to fixed terms grew, too, as the aging permanent delegates died off. Newly elected representatives tended to be well educated, reform-minded, and accountable to their constituencies. They injected new life into the geriatric parliament and subjected officials to unprecedentedly tough grilling. Taiwan's party and government were faced with a new concept: accountability.

The party-state itself suffered several humiliations in 1985. Revelations of the involvement of security officials in the murder of journalist Henry Liu in his Daly City, California, home in October 1984 elicited a storm of international criticism. A scandal involving the Taiwanese Cathay Group and top Finance Ministry officials forced several resignations and investigations. The PRC was achieving dramatic success with its bold reform policy, making Taiwan's conservatism look ludicrous. All this occurred at a time of a general economic downturn and lowered investor confidence. Meanwhile Chiang Ching-kuo's health was declining, and no clear successor had emerged. The party and state seemed undirected and lacking in vision.

There was an extraordinary breakthrough in 1986. Elections for the Legislative Yuan and National Assembly were scheduled for the end of the year. As the *dangwai* considered its strategy, Filipino People Power overthrew Ferdinand Marcos. The evidence that a seemingly invincible dictator could be ousted, and ousted peacefully at that, provided immeasurable inspiration to the Taiwanese opposition. In March the *dangwai's* proto-party, the Association of Public Policy Studies, established branches around the island. In the same month Chiang Ching-kuo established a task force to recommend reform measures, agreeing to let a group of liberal scholars mediate between the KMT and the opposition. Chiang clearly recognized that the

KMT needed to readjust its orientation; it could no longer command, but had to appeal for popular support like any other electorally oriented party.

On September 28, *dangwai* activists meeting at the Grand Hotel formally established the Democratic Progressive Party (DPP). Instead of prompting suppression, this illegal act spurred Chiang to tell the Central Standing Committee that new policies were needed to meet new challenges. The still illegal DPP took more than 20% of the popular vote in the 1986 elections.

The pace of reform accelerated. Chiang lifted martial law in July 1987. In November he permitted ROC citizens to make family visits to the mainland. Several hundred thousand Taiwanese took the chance to go touring, trading, and seeking investment opportunities as the authorities progressively eased the eligibility regulations.

President Chiang died on January 13, 1988. Under the terms of the constitution he was succeeded by Vice-President Lee Teng-hui. Lee also became chairman of the KMT. At the Thirteenth Party Congress in July, he brought more liberals into the leadership; a subsequent cabinet reshuffle brought more new, young faces into the government.

The lifting of martial law opened the floodgates to an overwhelming tide of social movements. Citizens organized groups concerned with consumer rights, the environment, women, aborigines, students, new religions, labor, farmers, teachers, the disadvantaged, political victims, mainlanders desiring to pay home visits, nuclear power, Hakka rights, stock market punters, and low-cost housing. Production was disrupted as the streets were regularly clogged with protest marchers. People began complaining about ultra-democracy; a demonstration of farmers protesting agricultural trade policy turned violent. Neither political party controlled this spontaneous politicization of society, though they both scrambled to co-opt the movements and claim the issues as their own.

In December 1989 Taiwan held the first multi-party elections in its history. Although the KMT won, the DPP scored dramatic gains. Some DPP candidates openly advocated Taiwanese independence, going so far as to publish a constitution for the new country. This patently illegal act went unpunished, and many of its advocates won decisively. Decades of shared education, culture, and improved living standards had not eradicated the rift between Taiwanese and mainlanders.

Clearly the electorate was concerned with the issue of Taiwan's identity and future, a question that made Beijing nervous. Though the PRC had abandoned its slogan of "liberating" Taiwan in 1979, it continued to press for "reunification of the motherland." Beijing proposed for Taiwan a "one country, two systems" formula similar to the one set for Hong Kong after July 1, 1997, but allowing Taiwan to retain even more autonomy. The PRC accompanied this carrot with a stick: it refused to renounce the use of force if Taiwan declared independence, if civil disorder broke out on the island, or if the authorities in Taipei linked up with the Soviet Union. One of Beijing's campaign tactics was to encourage mainland visits by people from Taiwan, but the policy backfired as the poverty and oppression of the mainland renewed the islanders' pride in Taiwan and their opposition to reunification.

Despite Lee Teng-hui's protestations of loyalty to reunification, his election to the presidency in March 1990 did little to allay the PRC's anxiety. The PRC wanted party-to-party talks; Lee, claiming that Taiwan had become a multi-party system, countered by proposing talks between the two governments as a way of compelling the PRC to acknowledge the continued existence of the ROC state. He also predicted a return to the mainland during his six-year term.

In May 1990 Lee nominated the unpopular Hau Po-tsun, the hardline chief of staff of the armed forces, as the premier. This appointment was seen as a sop to mainlanders skeptical of Lee's pro-reunification pronouncements. It was also meant to reassure business leaders concerned that strikes, demonstrations, rampant speculation in land and the stock market, underground investment houses, kidnapping, and crimes of violence were destroying Taiwan's reputation as a healthy business climate; investors were moving their operations offshore to Southeast Asia and mainland China. At the news of Hau's nomination, thousands of protestors who viewed the appointment as a thinly disguised return to martial law gathered at the Chiang Kai-shek Memorial Hall, Taiwan's Tiananmen Square.

Knowing that he could not adopt Beijing's solution of using the army to disperse demonstrators, Lee took a bold step. He convened a National Affairs Conference for the summer to discuss four outstanding issues: revision of the constitution, reform of parliament, reform of central and local government, and relations with the mainland. Lee hand-picked the 150 delegates, who included many DPP activists and former political prisoners, some of them released just prior to the Conference. He also promised to lift the Temporary Provisions, opening the door to fundamental reforms. The Conference aired these issues amid much publicity. Whether substantive reforms would emerge, however, remained unresolved.

Taiwan in the 1990's

Taiwan enters the final decade of the twentieth century facing some very tough challenges. On the economic front, Taiwan must upgrade its industrial structure to survive. Labor-intensive operations are no longer viable; taking advantage of a severe labor shortage and virtual full employment, available workers are bidding up wages so high that Taiwan is no longer competitive. The 1984 Labor Standard Law set a minimum wage of NT$ 8,000 a month; in mid-1988 actual monthly wages averaged NT$ 15,800. The government is debating the issue of importing labor from Southeast Asia and mainland China, although tens of thousands of people are working in Taiwan already without legal status. The shortage of workers has stalled progress on the fourteen current major infrastructural projects. With the lifting of martial law, disgruntled workers are free to strike, and labor activists are eager to help them. The stock market boom of the late 1980's drew laborers from the worksite to securities houses, where they earned more money faster. The work ethic suffers.

At the low end Taiwan faces severe competition from Southeast Asia and mainland China, where labor is cheap, abundant, and disciplined. These countries have adopted the Taiwanese model of export orientation and export processing zones. They are now beating Taiwan at its own game by attracting foreign investment—including hundreds of millions of dollars from Taiwan.

The New Taiwan dollar appreciated 40% between 1985 and 1989, raising costs and attracting a great deal of "hot money" from speculators hoping to make a killing on the currency's appreciation. Added to Taiwan's accumulated foreign exchange, which exceeded US$ 70 billion from 1987 to spring 1990, this infusion of capital created an inflationary spiral, especially in land. Local businessmen are finding it easier to make money on speculation than investment.

Taiwan faces continued protectionist sentiments in its main overseas markets. Taiwan is America's fifth largest trade partner, and although the figures have fallen, exports remain overly concentrated on the United States: 38% in 1988. Similarly, although the record $16 billion 1987 trade surplus with the United States has been reduced, it remains unacceptably high: $12 billion in 1989. Taiwan narrowly escaped inclusion on the Super 301 list of free trade violators in 1989. By contrast, the country runs a huge deficit with Japan (US$ 7 billion in 1989). Taiwan's challenge now is to diversify its sources of parts and components, upgrade the value-added component of its exports, and seek new outlets for exports. Many owners of labor-intensive industries have moved their operations offshore in search of cheap labor, hoping to continue to earn money from the same goods rather than invest in expensive automation equipment. Others have been driven out by a general perception of a breakdown in social order.

Social movements have zeroed in on some of the costs of Taiwan's headlong drive toward industrialization, focusing in particular on environmental degradation in the hope of blocking the establishment of new polluting factories and cleaning up existing ones. A new Environmental Protection Agency tries to enforce regulations, but meets resistance from investors.

Taiwan can reduce but never eliminate its dependence on imported oil and its dependence on exports. The Middle East crisis of 1990, sparked by Iraq's occupation of Kuwait, sent oil prices soaring. In Taiwan, as in so many other countries, the volatility of oil prices has a sharp impact on the health of the economy and the confidence of investors.

Politically, Lee Teng-hui must follow through on recommendations from the National Affairs Conference. Although many in the middle class decry the upsurge in political activity, the mobilized minority speaks to their common concern about the island's future, specifically the question of who should determine Taiwan's fate. The ROC has lost its international identity. Taiwan was the world's twelfth largest trading nation in 1989. Its citizens do business all over the world, yet they lack diplomatic protection, a constant, humiliating reminder of their government's political impotence.

Relations with the mainland are thus a primary factor in the Taiwan political and economic equation. Trade between Taiwan and the PRC reached US$ 3.7 billion in 1989. Outright Taiwanese investment on the mainland, all of it indirect and officially illegal, passed US$ 1 billion at the end of 1989. Hundreds of thousands of ROC passport holders have visited the PRC, and information about the mainland now pervades Taiwan. A material basis for relations is being established. Strengthened material relations, however, do not translate into Taiwanese support for reunification under any of the formulas presented so far. On the contrary, there is renewed sentiment for Taiwanese independence.

Clearly the KMT can no longer call the shots. It faces not only a small but vocal opposition party, but also a mobilized civil society taking matters into its own hands. Generational transition certainly means the end of mainlander monopoly, perhaps even of mainlander dominance. Liberal elements of the KMT may join with moderates in the DPP, or the KMT may split into open factions along the lines of Japan's Liberal Democratic Party. Taiwan no longer has strongmen like the Chiangs who can bring things back together.

The KMT cannot easily guide the economy into a new niche in the world system, nor can it command society to do its bidding. Restructuring will dominate the 1990's as the KMT readjusts its relation with society, social forces adjust their relations with each other, and the island faces accommodation with the mainland.

Singapore:
Developmental Paternalism

Frederic C. Deyo

The people of Singapore, like their counterparts in South Korea, Taiwan, and Hong Kong, have enjoyed dramatic economic gains over the past twenty-five years. Continuing rapid economic growth, eventuating in a per capita national income now rivaling that of New Zealand, Ireland, and Spain, has virtually eliminated previously high levels of unemployment and poverty. Most Singaporeans now enjoy adequate housing, excellent public education, cheap health care, and a nutritious diet.

Singapore's success story, however, goes well beyond economic growth. Far more than East Asians elsewhere, Singapore's citizens have been spared the indignities of crime, litter, drugs, traffic congestion, pollution, and other social ills visited upon city dwellers in developing and developed countries alike.

To a somewhat lesser degree than in South Korea and Taiwan, economic growth in Singapore has been guided by an authoritarian, interventionist state, relying in this instance on a large state enterprise sector on the one hand, and on selective inducement of direct foreign investment on the other. But more remarkable than the economic role of the state is its social development role. This role encompasses provision for social welfare, best exemplified by a comprehensive national pension scheme and a massive public housing program. It includes as well the preemptive creation of social organizations like trade unions, colleges, and local political institutions, and their incorporation into a hierarchically organized, state-directed structure through which to impose political controls and implement government policy. In addition, Lee Kuan Yew's People's Action Party (PAP) has directly intervened with sometimes draconian measures to reduce political dissent, violent crime, drug trafficking, traffic congestion, and other social problems. Finally, the state has sought, with some success, to penetrate and direct personal

Frederic Deyo teaches sociology at the State University of New York at Brockport. He has lived and taught in Singapore. His field of specialization is Asian industrialism and labor relations. His most recent books are *The Political Economy of the New Asian Industrialism* and *Beneath the Miracle: Labor Subordination of the New Asian Industrialism.*

Notes for this chapter can be found on pages 186–187.

and social life to a degree unprecedented in modern society, extending to such matters as hair length, language preference, and the marriage age of women.

Through ruthlessly efficient and comprehensive economic, political, and social engineering, Singapore's corruption-free government has created a prosperous, peaceful, and well-ordered society. But such comprehensive social engineering has created its own peculiar malaise—a sense that life is over-planned, too well ordered, too disciplined. Despite continuing economic growth and expanding career opportunities, large numbers of young, well-educated Singaporeans have chosen in recent years to emigrate from Singapore, citing dissatisfaction with work pressure and with political regulations and restrictions.

Insofar as Singapore's modern history defines possible upper limits to the scope and efficacy of national socio-economic planning, Singapore presents a unique and important case study of developmental state intervention. This chapter seeks to understand the way in which economic growth, society, and politics have influenced and been shaped by the PAP's energetic and intrusive developmental planning.

Colonialism and Post-Colonialism

When Sir Stamford Raffles, an agent for the East India Company, first established British control over Singapore harbor through an agreement with the then sultan of Johor in 1819, Singapore was little more than a sparsely populated and tiny island of jungle and swamp. Subsequent British development of the island, however, quickly transformed it into a rapidly growing port city handling a substantial volume of trade among Southeast Asian countries and between Asia and the West. Singapore's expanding *entrepot* role was given further impetus by the arrival of steam-powered boats in 1845, the Australian gold rush of the early 1850's, and the opening of the Suez Canal in 1869. Equally important was regional development of the tin and rubber industries of Malaya and Sumatra during the early 1900's. These industries, along with increased production of such other commodities as timber and plantation crops, bolstered Singapore's emerging role as a center for the processing and trans-shipment of regional products. At the same time the country developed related banking, shipping, insurance, and storage services.

In the decades that followed, growing numbers of immigrants flocked to Singapore to find work in shipyards, docks, clerical offices, small factories, commercial and financial enterprises, and government service. By 1931 the population had reached 558,000, 75% of whom were Chinese, 13% Malays, and 8% Indians. These figures understate the ethnic heterogeneity of Singapore. The Chinese consisted of various dialect groups, including especially Hokkien, Teochiu, and Cantonese. Similarly, the Malays included peninsular Malays, Javanese, and Boyanese, while the Indians brought with them distinct regional languages and cultures of India.

Interrupted only by the Japanese occupation during World War II, Singapore flourished as the *entrepot,* financial, and commercial center of peninsular and insular Southeast Asia throughout the 1950's. These activities were supplemented by shipbuilding and repair, much of it associated with the extensive British naval facilities in Singapore. In addition, unimpeded trade between Malaya and Singapore fostered growth in the domestic manufacture of goods for local markets.

In 1959 Singapore attained self-rule in internal affairs, although Great Britain retained control over foreign relations. Lee Kuan Yew's People's Action Party (PAP) emerged victorious from the elections leading up to the formation of the new government, drawing support particularly from leftist trade unions, Chinese-language associations, and anglicized nationalist moderates. During the post-election period, growing friction between leftists and moderates led to a formal split, with the leftists breaking away to form their own party, the Barisan Socialis, or Socialist Front. This split in the party was paralleled by the dissolution of the Singapore Trades Union Congress into a leftist federation, the Singapore Association of Trade Unions, and a moderate federation, the National Trades Union Congress, which retained affiliation with the PAP.

This political conflict extended to the ongoing debate about the future course of Singapore's economy. Of particular importance was the question of union with Malaya. Under the terms of an agreement negotiated by the PAP with Britain, full independence was to be granted Singapore as a constituent state of the larger Malaysian Federation. The agreement to seek entry into the federation met with strong opposition from Chinese leftists who feared their political role would be diluted in the larger Malay-dominated federation. It was this conflict which provided the impetus for the final elimination of Singapore's political Left as the PAP set out systematically to isolate and eliminate leftist opposition in trade unions, secondary schools, and elsewhere. After the 1963 general elections, in which the Barisan Socialis was defeated, the party was de-registered and a number of oppositional leaders were jailed during the ruthless mopping-up campaign known as "Operation Cold Store."

The PAP then turned to the tasks of merger and economic development. The Economic Development Board, established in 1961 to coordinate and implement economic planning, directed new initiatives to stimulate local manufacture for domestic consumption in the now enlarged federation common market formed by the federation with Malaya. Domestic industry received expanded tax incentives and tariff protection. Growth in manufacturing, along with continued strength in foreign-dominated petroleum refining, chemicals, and shipbuilding and repair, moved Singapore away from its earlier nearly exclusive reliance on *entrepot* trade and trans-shipment.

This economically smooth, if politically conflictive, transition from *entrepot* trade to Import Substitution Industrialization (ISI) was abruptly terminated in the mid-1960's. The most important reason for halting ISI was that growing political conflicts between Singapore's PAP and political groups in Malaya led to Singapore's expulsion from the new federation in 1965; Singapore lost access to Malaya's large domestic market, and with it the viability of an import-substituting plan of industrialization. In addition, in 1968 British authorities announced that by 1971 they would close the huge British naval facilities in Singapore, which employed nearly 20% of the local work force and accounted for 13% of total Gross Domestic Product. Its economic policy thus thrown into disarray, the PAP faced an economic crisis underlined by growing unemployment, which reached 9.2% in 1966. It was in this context that the PAP adopted a new export-oriented development strategy that was to profoundly transform the social, political, and economic life of this small island republic.

Export-Oriented Industrialization

In 1965 Singapore faced a very uncertain future. The range of practicable responses to the economic crisis was limited by the island's very small domestic market, now confined to the island itself, its few mineral resources, small agricultural sector, very weak domestic industrial bourgeoisie, and lack of access to significant foreign assistance. On the other hand, Singapore's well situated and developed port facility, in conjunction with its abundant and comparatively well educated domestic work force, suggested a strategy of labor-intensive Export Oriented Industrialization (EOI). Such a strategy in turn implied a return to the free-trade regime of earlier, colonial years.

The choice of an appropriate mix of local private companies, state enterprises, and foreign firms to spearhead industrial development was in part determined by a general perception that the entrepreneurial sector could not respond quickly to the requirements of rapid industrialization. This weakness in the domestic industrial bourgeoisie was in part a legacy of earlier British support for the financial and other service industries most closely linked to *entrepot* trade, resulting in a relative lack of attention to the development of local manufacturing. In addition, Singapore's very short and abruptly terminated period of ISI had failed to provide the prolonged nurturing enjoyed by local industry in Taiwan and South Korea. The new export strategy therefore seemed to dictate reliance on direct foreign investment to foster rapid industrialization.

The new strategy called as well for forceful government measures in order to mobilize and effectively use the one significant resource Singapore did possess, abundant human labor. Indeed, Singapore's development policy over subsequent decades was to center on the successful marriage of local labor with foreign capital.

Singapore's economic development has been led by three groups of institutional actors: government statutory boards, public enterprises, and foreign companies. Statutory boards, mandated to implement socio-economic development plans formulated within planning units of the ministries of finance and trade and industry, have provided the foundation for state-led industrialization. Their various functions include promotion of investment, development of infrastructure and essential services, public housing and urban redevelopment, education, promotion of tourism, development of Singapore as a financial center, family planning, and promotion of sports and recreational activities. The statutory boards, while substantially independent of government control in personnel, finance, and external dealings, control roughly two-thirds of all development expenditure and are the instruments of nearly all government development programs.

The most important of these boards, the Economic Development Board (EDB), was established on the recommendation of an advisory United Nations mission during 1960–61. The EDB was empowered to administer industrial incentives to promoted industries, underwrite stock issues, grant loans to or purchase equity participation in industrial enterprises, acquire or lease land for and develop industrial sites, and provide training and other forms of assistance to firms. This board's primary developmental mandate was to reduce unemployment, a goal associated with the promotion of foreign investment in labor-intensive production. The EDB's preoccupation with facilitating foreign investment and its corresponding lack of attention to domestic industry set Singapore apart from most other developing Asian societies.

Some of the EDB's functions eventually devolved to newly created, more specialized bodies. The Jurong Town Corporation, for example, was established in 1968 to develop and manage industrial estates; its responsibilities include land acquisition, resettlement, estate housing, and port development.

The Housing Development Board, another statutory board, was established in 1960 to create and administer public housing programs. It accomplished this primarily by constructing massive new housing estates scattered across the island.

Singapore's public housing scheme, which now accommodates 86% of the population, is the most ambitious such program in the capitalist world.

Another statutory board, the Central Provident Fund (CPF), has played a key role in mobilizing domestic savings for local investment. A mandatory national pension program based on payroll taxes payable by employers and employees, the CPF has contributed substantially to Singapore's achieving the highest savings rate in the world. In 1984 public sector gross savings accounted for fully 64% of total Gross National Savings, in large measure because of the CPF and the Post Office Savings Bank. The CPF alone contributed 17% of Gross National Savings in 1985. These savings are used to underwrite massive public investments in infrastructure and housing.

The second important instrument of government development policy is public enterprise. Under the Ministry for Finance Incorporation Act of 1959, the government established the legal basis for equity participation in private-sector firms. Through equity shareholding by the government, statutory boards, or such holding companies as the Development Bank of Singapore and Sembawang Holdings, the government controls more than 160 local manufacturing and service sector companies. Public equity investment is typically directed to firms closely related to the developmental interests of government; the state has large investments in petrochemicals, iron and steel, engineering, shipbuilding, shipping, finance, and tourism. In addition, the government channels public investment to developmentally important industries which have failed to attract investment from foreign or local investors, or in which foreign capital domination is undesirable for security or other reasons.

The third key to rapid economic growth is foreign capital, which dominates the economy of Singapore more than that of any other Third World nation. By providing low-cost sites, nearby public housing for workers, and excellent infrastructure, including good port facilities, the EDB, Jurong Town Corporation, Housing Development Board, and other statutory boards greatly reduced the time and money foreign firms needed to start up local operations. The EDB also provided a highly efficient one-stop servicing office for processing investment applications. EDB-administered investment incentives established in 1959 allowed 100% foreign ownership and full repatriation of profits. The Economic Expansion Act of 1967 offered in addition a range of new tax incentives including accelerated depreciation, duty-free importation of equipment and inputs, and a large reduction in taxes on exports of approved products.

The Economic Expansion Act disproportionately favored foreign investors, who were better placed than local firms by virtue of the size of their export capacity to take advantage of its incentives. More important, while earlier foreign investment had targeted such capital-intensive industries as oil refining and chemicals, new capital inflows were directed to labor-intensive, export-oriented industries targeted by the EDB: textiles, footwear and leather, transport equipment, electrical machinery, and electronics.

So rapid was the inflow of foreign capital after 1967 that by 1975 foreign firms absorbed 76% of total manufacturing inputs, produced 71% of total outputs, and accounted for 65% of all capital formation in manufacturing. By the mid-1980's these firms employed fully half the work force, produced 70% of total output, and accounted for 80% of total investment commitments in manufacturing. More important, foreign firms accounted for an ever greater percentage of manufactured exports, the core of the new development strategy. These firms accounted for 55.3% of manufactured exports in 1970, 70% in the late 1970's, and more than 90% in the early 1980's.

The employment consequences of the influx of foreign investment, particularly in electronics, were equally dramatic. Indeed, employment generation in the new industries was so rapid that by the mid-1970's concerns about unemployment were replaced by a growing apprehension of labor shortages. Between 1966 and 1974 manufacturing employment increased from 19.0% to 28.5% of total employment, and accounted for 47% of total employment growth during this period. Much of this increase centered on low-skill assembly production by foreign companies like Hewlett-Packard, Fairchild, Rollei, Hitachi, and General Electric. New investments by companies like these were largely responsible for the doubling of manufacturing employment between 1968 and 1971 alone.

The work force generated by this new investment consisted primarily of young, single women. Between 1970 and 1974 the number of female production workers in manufacturing increased by 48,500, nearly doubling total female employment in this sector. In 1974, 71% of female production workers were below the age of 29, and 26% were below 19. These young women were the primary source of the cheap labor required for competitive export manufacturing during this early stage of EOI.

The extraordinary inflow of foreign capital cannot be fully explained by economic incentives, infrastructural development, and Singapore's strategic location. Singapore's economic incentives, usually cited as the key to foreign investment, may in fact be of only secondary importance to potential investors. A recent survey of foreign firms reported that the most important single factor underlying their decision to locate in Singapore was political stability. And of all the government policies and measures that foreign managers regarded as important to their operations in Singapore, labor relations policy outranked tax and other industrial incentives.

By the late 1960's the PAP was already able to provide credible assurance to foreign investors that their Singapore operations would confront neither political uncertainty nor labor militancy. The defeat of the Left by the mid-1960's eliminated the only viable opposition to stable PAP rule. It also provided the basis for a final assault on union militancy. Of particular importance were two new labor laws enacted in 1968. The Employment Act reduced permissible retrenchment payments, overtime work, bonuses, maternity and holiday leave, and fringe benefits, thus slowing increases in non-wage compensation. The Industrial Relations Act was even more important, especially in reducing the acrimony and expense of collective bargaining, in giving management full discretionary power in matters of promotion, transfer, recruitment, dismissal, reinstatement, assignment or allocation of duties, and termination by reason of reorganization or redundancy. None of these decisions was any longer subject to bargaining. If high levels of union militancy in the early 1960's had been brought down by the political defeat of the Left, continuing moderate levels of conflict were now further reduced by the legislative removal of many issues from collective bargaining altogether.

Domestic firms were playing an increasingly marginal developmental role by the mid-1970's. This decline has been furthered by a general absence of government performance requirements for foreign investors. Unlike Taiwan and South Korea, where foreign investment in many sectors is restricted to minority ownership, profit repatriation is controlled, and foreign firms are obliged to meet domestic content and export requirements, Singapore places few such requirements on foreign investors. Nearly one-half of foreign-invested firms in Singapore are wholly owned subsidiaries of overseas corporations. These firms import most of their required supplies and equipment rather than purchasing them locally, ostensibly because local suppliers cannot meet their quality and delivery requirements. In addition, established foreign companies are well placed to outbid smaller domestic firms for local capital and skilled workers. Given these circumstances, it is not surprising that domestic companies failed substantially to benefit from the inflow of foreign capital.

The progressive decline of domestic industry has drawn repeated complaints from local business associations. In 1977 the Chinese Chamber of Commerce and Industry issued a public report arguing that domestic firms were being squeezed by foreign firms, by government policies which seemed to favor foreign over domestic firms, and by government enterprises themselves. In support of the latter claim the

Chamber submitted a list of more than one hundred state-owned firms that competed directly with private companies. This bypassing of domestic economic forces in the island's development was to create unanticipated obstacles to continued growth.

Economic Restructuring

Singapore's policy of EOI based on light industry faced increasing constraints during the 1970's. The oil shocks of the mid- and late 1970's slowed growth in world markets. More important, access to export markets became increasingly problematic as industrialists and trade unions in the United States and elsewhere demanded protection from a growing flood of imports from low-wage Asian countries. In response to these demands the United States removed Singapore and the other East Asian newly industrializing countries from its list of countries entitled to preferential import duties. The increase in American tariffs that went into effect in January 1989 is expected to substantially reduce the competitiveness of a number of Singapore's exports to the United States.

In addition to external problems, growing labor shortages and corresponding upward wage pressure at home in the 1970's posed a fundamental challenge to an export strategy predicated on cheap local labor. As employers encountered increasing difficulty in recruiting workers for low-wage factory work, investment capital began to seek alternative, lower-cost production sites. In the short term these pressures were partially alleviated by continued growth in female employment. In the peak employment ages of 20 to 24 years, female labor force participation increased from 54% in 1970 to 78% in 1980 and 81% in 1988. Employment rates increased even more dramatically for older women, in part because of declining fertility and greater provision of child-care facilities in housing estates. The liberalization of Singapore's immigration policy provided a second short-term solution to the problem of labor shortages. During the mid- to late 1980's it has been estimated that about 150,000 foreign workers (12% of the work force, mostly from Malaysia) held jobs in construction and other labor-intensive industries. At the same time it became clear that a more fundamental policy change was necessary for the longer run.

In response to the growing threats to continued economic growth, the PAP sought to encourage a shift away from low-skill, labor-intensive manufacturing toward higher-value-added production employing more highly skilled workers. The government calculated that such a shift would permit productivity gains to keep pace with rising wages, thus stabilizing unit labor costs and maintaining Singapore's global competitiveness. Indeed, this shift in government industrial policy had begun as early as 1970, when Singapore stopped providing special "pioneer" status to industries engaged primarily in simple assembly operations. In subsequent years the government redirected investment incentives to consumer electronics, precision instruments, pharmaceuticals, and such non-manufacturing industries as engineering, communications, finance, health care, and other modern service industries. Within established industries, the government sought to encourage increased research and development, mechanization, and automation through major incentives such as a five- to ten-year exemption from corporate profit taxes.

Government economic restructuring efforts relied only in part on incentives and industrial policy, however. As it had in its earlier efforts to attract foreign investment, the PAP made important changes in labor policy relating to training and education, wages, and labor relations. In an effort to improve skill levels and productivity, the government has invested heavily in expanded technical education. This investment is reflected in substantial increases in government educational expenditures after 1979 as well as in a sharp growth in enrollment in vocational and technical programs in high schools, colleges, and various training programs such as those offered at EDB Joint Industrial Training Centers. Between 1977 and 1984 government expenditures for education increased from 14.5% to 20.2% of total government expenditures, with much of the increase going to technical and vocational studies. In 1977, 7.8% of all high school teachers were vocational teachers; by 1987 the percentage had risen to 15.3%. During the same period the percentage of high school students enrolled in vocational curricula increased from 19% to 28.4%.

The Skills Development Fund, a payroll levy used to reimburse firms for approved worker training programs, provided further incentive for company training. The National Productivity Board has also provided training support by creating quality control circles and by sponsoring technical seminars and workshops.

More dramatic was a change in wage policy in the late 1970's. Starting in the early 1970's, a tripartite National Wages Council issued annual wage guidelines for wage negotiations. After 1973, when wages were allowed to rise gradually in order to discourage further investment in low-skill assembly production, these guidelines were highly restrictive. But in 1979, in line with new efforts to restructure the economy, the guidelines recommended a full 20% across-the-board wage increase. This increase was followed by additional large increments in 1980 and 1981. The government viewed this highly controversial policy shift, which in fact was partially blamed by commentators for later economic problems, as a key element in its restructuring efforts.

The final change in labor policy centered on trade unions. During the early

1970's the PAP had supported the creation of a powerful, highly centralized national trade union federation. Closely aligned with the ruling party, the National Trades Union Congress (NTUC) had supported government labor policy, encouraging wage restraint, productivity increases, training, and other national economic programs. NTUC membership increased rapidly during this early period in response to proliferation of a wide range of highly attractive member services. During the restructuring effort ten years later, however, this centralized union organization became increasingly anachronistic. The government decided that house unions would better serve to increase the stability of the labor force, encourage workers to be loyal to their companies, and stimulate greater employer investment in worker training and increased productivity. In 1982 the two largest NTUC union affiliates were accordingly broken into smaller industry-based unions, while house unions were set up in several public enterprises and given strong encouragement in the private sector. By 1985 thirty-five of the eighty-four unions in Singapore were house unions; only ten of these, however, had been established since 1982. The encouragement of house unions implied no relaxation in government control. Indeed, the PAP increased its control over unions by increasing the discretionary power of the Registrar of Trade Unions over union registration, strengthening the supervisory powers of the NTUC leadership, the Labour Ministry, and the Registrar of Societies over union activities and finance, and establishing closer links between the NTUC and the PAP. In addition, the Trade Union Act of 1982 assigned unions a greater role in promoting productivity and cooperation with management. In full acceptance of their renewed responsibilities, unions helped to implement the 1984 Employment Act, which gave management increased flexibility and discretion in the organization of production.

At the same time that unions were being decentralized, firms were permitted to hold back a portion of their mandatory CPF contributions and to use these savings to set up employee welfare funds. Along with house unions, enterprise-based welfare benefits were intended on the one hand to increase workers' enterprise loyalty and productivity, and on the other to encourage employers to be more willing to finance costly worker training in the expectation that reduced worker turnover would ensure a fuller return on their training investments.

Union membership declined sharply as centralized union structures gave way to smaller industry- and enterprise-based unions and growing enterprise paternalism. Between 1978 and 1984 NTUC membership declined from 31% to 22% of the organizable work force. This decline followed in part from rapid employment growth in new, smaller firms in high-technology and service sectors. However, it also reflected the government's reduced efforts to organize industrial workers into state-controlled unions and its greater reliance on local labor-management negotiation in union formation and recognition.

The government's restructuring efforts resulted in moderate changes in industrial structure from the mid-1970's onward. Growth in electronics (especially personal computers and semiconductors), precision equipment, and pharmaceuticals, for example, outpaced textiles and other traditional labor-intensive industries. Accompanying these changes in manufacturing structure was a corresponding shift into modern services, especially finance, engineering, and business consultancy. Beginning in 1980, in fact, the trends of the 1970's were reversed as financial and business services grew faster than manufacturing. Between 1973 and 1985 the work force in financial services alone increased from 3.6% to 8.6% of total employment.

But the decade of the 1980's was not one of uninterrupted economic growth. Global economic stagnation in the early 1980's, especially in the United States, Singapore's most important export market, was reflected in weaker growth domestically. Shipbuilding and electronics were especially hard hit. There was a far deeper recession in 1985 and 1986, when real Gross Domestic Product declined by 1.6% and 1.8% respectively. Growth rates returned to levels above 8% in subsequent years, with corresponding increases in employment and renewed upward pressure on wages.

The mid-1980's recession forced the government's awareness of Singapore's longer-term vulnerability from over-reliance on foreign investment, on a few key export industries, and on a few overseas markets. Initially attracted to Singapore by its low wages, excellent infrastructure, and political stability, foreign investors responded less than enthusiastically to the government's restructuring efforts. In many cases they simply moved production to cheaper countries as the island's rising labor costs became increasingly uncompetitive. Japanese and other foreign firms redirected new investments to Malaysia, Thailand, and other countries in the region. American-based General Electric, at ten thousand employees the largest private-sector employer in Singapore in the early 1980's, cut local employment by half as part of its worldwide restructuring in the mid-1980's.

A second goal of the government's restructuring effort was to encourage greater technology transfer and the relocation to Singapore of research and development facilities. Foreign firms were unresponsive. Technology transfer was limited, and there was virtually no increase in the number of foreign firms engaging in significant research and development activities in Singapore between 1980 and 1985. The preponderance of government over private investment in research and development is indicative of the weakness of the foreigners' response; in 1984 government funding totalled 105 million Singapore dollars, private funding only 92 million Singapore dollars.

Singapore's rapid economic growth from 1982 to 1984 depended less on manufactured exports than on growth in construction and services, and disguised the economy's fundamental vulnerability from over-dependence on foreign investment. The cost of foreign dependence became clearer during 1985–86, when economic stagnation, the consequence in part of a worldwide economic slowdown and the completion of earlier construction projects, was made even worse by sharp investment cutbacks by foreign companies.

Another of the government's incentives to redirect economic policy was its recognition of the dangers of relying too heavily on a few export industries (electronics, shipbuilding, and oil) and on a few export markets in developed countries (especially the United States, which absorbs roughly one-third of total exports). The disk drive industry is a case in point. Singapore is the world's largest producer of disk drives, which in turn are Singapore's largest non-oil export item. In response to a downturn in demand in the United States, the major market for this product, leading producers like Seagate Technology have been cutting back production and employment. This industry plays such a significant role in Singapore's economy that these cutbacks have significantly depressed exports, and exports are the key to Singapore's economic growth.

At the height of the 1985 recession, the PAP established a special Economic Committee headed by Lee Kuan Yew's son, Lee Hsien Loong, to assess the causes of the recession and propose fundamental changes in economic policy. Pursuant to the recommendations of this committee, the government undertook a number of policy initiatives in subsequent years. Policies were designed to encourage foreign firms to take fuller advantage of Singapore's excellent telecommunications infrastructure, highly educated work force, and strategic location by establishing regional headquarters on the island. Two American-based firms, Texas Instruments and Data General, have begun to do so. At the same time the government is trying to establish special cheap-labor zones to which companies can move labor-intensive production operations while keeping their head offices in Singapore; the PAP is negotiating with Indonesia, for example, to create such an industrial zone on the nearby island of Batam. Related efforts to establish Singapore as a regional agribusiness production and distribution center began in 1988 with the funding of several new agro-industrial parks. And new tax incentives are designed to speed the shift already underway from manufacturing to service activities. Significantly, the government has departed from its traditional stance on foreign investment by imposing strict foreign ownership restrictions in three such service industries: banking, transport, and the media.

The government has sought to increase the competitiveness of private-sector firms by cutting business taxes from 40 to 31% and by temporarily reducing mandatory employer CPF contribution rates from 25% to 10%. And, reversing its earlier wage policy, the government has renewed efforts to rein in wages. In 1986 fifty unions responded to a call for wage restraint by voluntarily giving up pay increases already agreed on under National Wages Council guidelines.

The Economic Committee recognized that heavy-handed state economic intervention was no longer either appropriate or effective. "Circumstances," noted the committee's report,

> have now changed. The economy is larger, and the private sector is more developed....But the government is unlikely to have the detailed and omniscient grasp of all sectors to identify which project to put money on, even if it knows which areas should be promoted. New investments, and with them the impetus for growth, have to be the responsibility of the private sector.

In accordance with this new emphasis on the private sector, the government adopted a policy of gradual privatization of the very large state enterprise sector, starting with the limited public sale of equity shares in Singapore Airlines. Another incentive for the government to re-energize domestic firms has been the apparent reluctance of foreign companies, especially Japanese, to initiate substantial local research and development or to introduce in their Singapore operations the high technology they employ at home.

Politics in Singapore: Confucian Developmental Paternalism

Concern for political stability is a near obsession for Lee and other PAP leaders. Their preoccupation is most apparent in the government's seeming overreaction to even minimal political opposition. From 1968 to 1980 the ruling party won every seat in four national parliamentary elections and numerous by-elections. In 1981, however, Joshua Jeyaretnam, a Sri Lankan-born lawyer and leader of the Workers' Party, won a parliamentary by-election, and two opposition M.P.'s were elected in 1984. The loss of these seats to opposition parties was accompanied by a moderate erosion in the PAP's share of the popular vote; its 78% share in 1980 fell to 65% in 1984 and 63.1% in 1988. After the 1984 elections produced one opposition M.P., Lee questioned whether the principle of "one man, one vote" might have to be compromised in the interest of political stability. First Deputy Prime Minister Goh Chok Tong remarked in this regard on the insufficiency of capable and qualified leaders in so small a republic for successful multi-party government. And following the release of electoral survey data showing a disproportionate lack of support among younger first-time voters, Lee even suggested the possibility of granting voters over the age of forty a double vote "because they [had] lived longer."

Such overreaction to a slight decline in voters' support does not seriously detract from the the PAP's record of remarkable electoral support over a twenty-year period. To what may we attribute such success? The answer is to be found in Singapore's rapid economic growth and improved social welfare, the repression of domestic opposition, the effective incorporation of potential opposition groups into the ruling party, and the systematic encouragement of a supportive national ideology.

Singapore's phenomenal economic growth rate, one of the highest in the world during the 1970's, afforded substantial improvements in social welfare. In part such improvements followed from economic expansion itself and corresponding gains for workers. From 1977 to 1987 unemployment averaged about 4%, rising to 6% only in 1986, near the end of a recession. Singapore's per capita income in 1987 stood at US$ 8,289, higher than Spain's and Ireland's and equal to New Zealand's. Wages have increased rapidly during the 1980's, and income distribution, though it has slipped somewhat in recent years, is relatively equitable by international standards. More general indicators of quality of life support this picture of broad-based economic improvement. Infant mortality rates declined from 12.4 per thousand in 1977 to 7.4 in 1987. At 76.3 for females and 70.0 for males, life expectancy is comparable to that in the industrialized countries.

Beyond these positive consequences of economic growth, government social policy has further enhanced public welfare. Singapore is no welfare state, and indeed avoids public relief: there is no provision for unemployment compensation. One earns one's way on this industrial island. On the other hand, public housing estates accommodate 86% of the population, public health facilities are plentiful and cheap, and a national pension plan ensures sufficient savings for retirement. Companies and trade unions are required to provide for the safety and welfare of their members. Wage increases have been actively promoted during the 1980's. And public recreational and social facilities are subsidized and encouraged by the government. How does the PAP reconcile its tough attitude toward unemployment and public relief with its expansive social programs? The explanation is to be found in the fact that Singapore, more than the other East Asian newly industrializing countries, systematically uses social policy as an instrument of economic policy.

During the 1960's and early 1970's cheap, abundant labor emerged as the major developmental asset of this small island republic. Wage restraint and the curtailment of oppositional unionism were consequently the central pillars of labor policy. But even in those early years of PAP rule, government commitment to social welfare was manifest in Singapore's massive public housing program and the island-wide provision of public health services. The housing program in particular flowed in part from early electoral competition from which the PAP came to power on a platform promising public housing. Partly, however, the housing program has supported the economic goals of this "developmental state." In the early years of development public housing and other social services acted as an indirect wage subsidy, reducing the cost of living and thereby restraining wage pressure. In addition, the movement of the population out of *kampongs,* the traditional semi-rural housing of Singapore, and into high-rise rental housing both eliminated non-cash sources of income and necessitated new sources of cash income to pay rent. These new pressures forced many people who had previously been unemployed, particularly young women, into the work force. Finally, new housing estates were located near, or incorporated space for, light industry, thus concentrating new sources of employment near densely settled populations. In these ways the massive housing program may be seen as more than just a political response to earlier electoral pressure. After the final elimination of the Left, public housing became an instrument of development policy itself.

Restructuring increased the compatibility of proactive social policy and economic development. Throughout the modern period of industrialization, and especially after the mid-1970's, government developmental intervention sought to enhance the value and productivity of labor in order to attract investment and boost export competitiveness. Indeed, active encouragement of wage increases was seen as a way of speeding up this economic transition. Furthermore, since Singapore's development strategy is based on the island's human resources, public investment in education and health yields high returns. By 1985 over 80% of total government social expenditure was committed to education and health, the categories of "human capital investment" with the greatest and most direct return. Spending on education and vocational training has grown faster than any other category of social expenditure.

Near full employment, rising wages, provision of adequate housing and education, inexpensive public health services, and the virtual elimination of poverty provide an important basis for continued electoral support for the PAP. Indeed, they underpin the party's claim to socialist credentials. But where economic legitimation has not sufficed to silence the PAP's critics, political repression has provided a second, more sinister, foundation for political stability.

In consolidating its rule during the 1960's, the PAP eliminated its leftist opposition. While assuming more subtle forms, repression continues in modern Singapore. Public criticism of government policy typically draws a quick and harsh response. Opposition candidates who directly attack PAP officials or policy often face post-election lawsuits. After the 1986 conviction and imprisonment of Joshua Jeyaretnam, M.P., for falsifying the accounts of his party, the PAP passed a new law permitting M.P.'s to be jailed for making unsubstantiated charges against the government in or out of parliament.

Legislation presented for debate by parliament is open for questions and debate only upon its second reading, and debate is typically confined to only one day. Increasingly aggressive debate from young backbencher M.P.'s in the early 1980's led Deputy Prime Minister Goh to issue a public warning about irresponsible parliamentary behavior.

The PAP strictly controls the mass media. The government-owned Singapore Broadcasting Corporation controls all local television and radio broadcasting to ensure responsible reportage and editorial material, and can veto the appointment of key personnel in broadcasting. Criticism of the government in the press has led to the shutdown of local newspapers. In recent years the government has applied circulation restrictions to *Time, Asiaweek,* the *Asian Wall Street Journal,* and the *Far Eastern Economic Review* after they published articles critical of government policy. In 1990 the government even considered a new press law under which any foreign publication selling more than three hundred copies in Singapore of any issue that makes "any remarks, observations or comments pertaining to the politics and current affairs of any country in Southeast Asia" would have to obtain a government permit before it can circulate in the republic.

Students who are involved in politics in Singapore may be arrested and jailed, as in fact happened following student participation in worker protests during the 1974–75 recession. From 1964 to 1978 student applicants had to obtain "suitability certificates" (police guarantees of their political background) as a prerequisite for admission to the University of Singapore. More recently student union representatives at the university have been constitutionally prohibited from "engag[ing] in or mak[ing] pronouncements of a political nature."

Singapore's criminal justice system is harsh. Many criminal violations are punishable by rattan beatings. Under Singapore's strict internal security laws, political dissidents may be jailed indefinitely without trial. Chia Thye Poh was a Barisan Socialis M.P. until 1966, when he was arrested along with other opposition leaders. He has been in police custody for twenty-four years without trial. Many such prisoners have been released after public confessions of their political crimes. This was the experience of twenty-two dissidents who were arrested by the Internal Security Department in May and June 1987, and who were released only after televised confessions that they were indeed communist conspirators. Several of those released were again detained after they publicly repudiated their confessions, claiming they had been physically abused during custody. Having never consented to such a confession, Chia Thye Poh has not been released, but he has apparently outlasted his captors in patience. In 1989 the Internal Security Department moved

Singapore

The new overshadows the old in
the Singapore panorama.

The modern city reaching into
the sky.

Statue of Sir Stamford Raffles,
founder of the 1819 British
trading post on Singapore island.

A view of Singapore and the harbor, October, 1945.

A young girl dresses in an elaborate costume to celebrate a festival.

During Thimithi, the Fire Walking Festival at Sri Mariamman Temple, devotees walk across a four-meter pit glowing with burning coals.

Malay boys compete in a game of marbles.

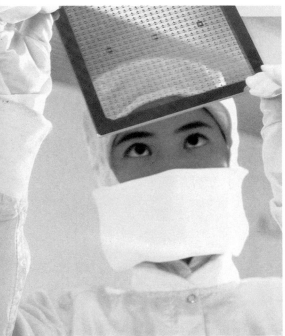

A state-of-the-art wafer diffusion and microchip design center has been set up in Singapore by the SGS Group of Italy.

A woodcarver produces gilded statuary for the market.

A Singapore street shop that offers dried peppers and other produce.

Family at a balcony window of a Malay housing compound.

An older street with residences above the shops.

Moslem women at prayer in a Singapore mosque.

A temple sculpture overlooks junks in the Singapore River.

A significant factor in Singapore's economic strength is the continued availability of well-prepared professionals from its institutions of higher education.

The Computer Graphic Centre at the National Technological Institute.

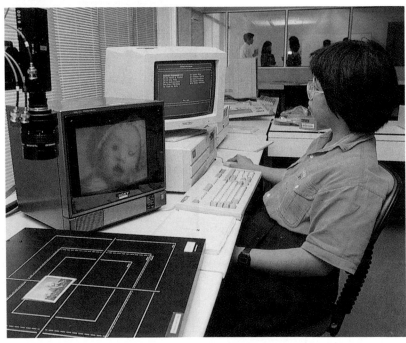

The clock tower of Victoria Theater and Concert Hall rises above buildings of colonial Singapore.

Tampines Junior College, one of 14 junior colleges in Singapore.

Singapore's skyline viewed from its modern port facility.

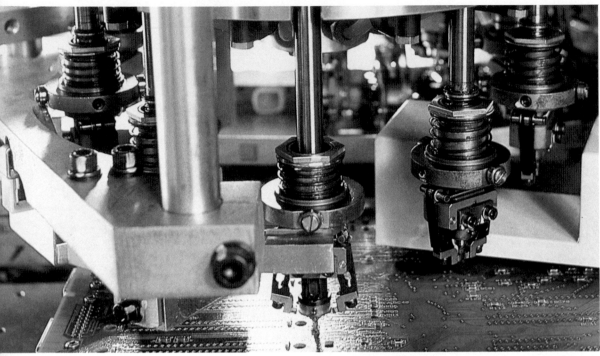

Robotic machining of electronic circuits.

An old-style Singapore barber shop.

Precision testing is used to verify that components meet standards.

Original species of tropical plants can still be found in Bukit Timah Nature Reserve.

Quality control circles take responsibility for continuous improvement of manufactured products.

A Chinese calligrapher demonstrates his art.

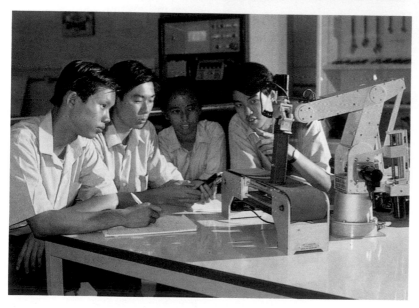

Trainees in the electro-mechanical servicing course at Jurong Vocational Institute learn about robotics.

A temple in Singapore's Chinatown.

The Singapore International Monetary Exchange, which is linked directly to the Chicago Mercantile Exchange.

When in 1959 Singapore was granted self-rule in internal affairs, Lee Kuan Yew became Singapore's Prime Minister; he retired from office in 1990, though he has stayed on as adviser and as head of the ruling party.

Sign in Changi Prison, Singapore.

Abandoned structures across the
Singapore River contrast with this
modern hotel.

Chettiar Hindu Temple,
Singapore.

him from his jail cell to Sentosa, an island amusement park off Singapore's coast, where he is now confined to a souvenir stand from which he sells local souvenirs to visiting tourists.

Singapore's political controls go far beyond crude repression. Indeed, Singapore's adherence to parliamentary forms and its relative lack of reliance on police coercion stand in marked contrast to South Korea and Taiwan, where martial law has played so important a role. In Singapore political corporatism and ideological legitimation have been far more important than repression. The PAP has created an extensive network of social organizations that link local populations to the ruling party. The most important of these are the People's Association and its network of community centers, residential organizations in public housing estates, Citizens' Consultative Committees, and the National Trades Union Congress.

The People's Association, chaired by the prime minister, is a statutory board established in 1960 to oversee social and cultural life in the republic. As stated in its charter, the objectives of the association are to promote group participation in social, cultural, educational, and athletic activities for the people of Singapore in order that they may realize that they belong to a multi-racial community, the interests of which transcend sectional loyalties; [and to establish] such institutions as may be necessary for the purpose of leadership training in order to instill in leaders a sense of national identity and a spirit of dedicated service to [the] community. In pursuit of these objectives the People's Association oversees the activities of approximately two hundred community centers, numerous social organizations, and a National Youth Leadership Training Institute through which community organization leaders are identified and trained.

Singapore's vast public housing program destroyed local, ethnically homogeneous *kampongs* and their replacement by government-organized housing projects. The informal solidarities of shared ethnicity, kinship, and cross-generational cooperation were replaced by the minimal, instrumental, and shallow interactions that characterize high-rise social life. In response to the attendant problems of crime and social disorder, the government has established a number of local organizations, including residents' committees and neighborhood watch schemes. Residents' committees, launched in 1978 and numbering more than 250 by 1985, have received substantial government support and publicity in recent years. Working closely with police, they function to maintain public order and promote social integration. Their importance to the enforcement of Housing Development Board rules is also clear. The board has significant legal power to discipline tenants who violate laws or engage in antisocial behavior; violations can result in penalties, eviction, and the barring of violators from access to public housing for five years.

But high-rise living creates circumstances in which the identification of offenders is difficult. The government-appointed residents' committees greatly facilitate the enforcement of Housing Development Board rules. In recognition of their success in reducing petty crime, Prime Minister Lee noted in 1984 that before the establishment of the committees, it had been very difficult to contain such anti-social behavior as throwing trash out of housing estate windows.

The prime minister's office also administers a network of Citizens' Consultative Committees, one in each parliamentary constituency. Committee members are government appointees, and meetings are run by local PAP M.P.'s. Under 1988 legislation the consultative committees, which provide a forum for public discussion of political issues, are soon to be joined by an additional network of constituency-based town councils.

In addition to performing their official duties, these organizations serve a clear political role. Peter Chen, a noted student of social change in Singapore, describes their function:

> Formal modern community organizations…which are sponsored and controlled by the Government, have emerged to replace the roles played by the traditional organizations…. The Government-based community organizations play the role not only of promoting community activities and of providing community services, but also of mobilizing the mass population in supporting government policies.

The NTUC, which encompasses most trade unions and the vast majority of total union membership, plays a similar role in preempting and channeling dissent and extending PAP control to the work place. Like the residential community organizations, the NTUC provides a forum for discussion of social issues, discipline of recalcitrant members, and the promotion of government policy.

These corporatist institutions draw their strength in part from the access they provide to social services and benefits. The People's Association sponsors and subsidizes the activities of the social activities of the organizations it oversees. Citizens' Consultative Committees provide a variety of services to local community residents. And NTUC affiliation affords access to a broad range of cooperative services for union members, including food retailing, travel services, public transport and taxis, consumer protection, books and stationery, and dental and health care.

Political corporatism both facilitates and is supported by the systematic development of a national ideology. Through these corporatist institutions and a government-regulated mass media, the PAP has propagated a rigid public morality stressing cleanliness, personal appearance, appropriate musical tastes, political loyalty, hard work, healthy living, and limited family size. Such values are frequently promoted through well organized and strongly funded national campaigns. Beginning in 1958 with the Anti-Spitting Campaign, the Kill Pests Campaign, and Operation Big-Sweep (anti-litter), dozens of campaigns have been channeled through the government-controlled press, community organizations, the NTUC, and other media; they have been enforced by police surveillance and incrementally applied legal penalties. The campaign against jaywalking, for instance, was accompanied by the legal prosecution of more than ten thousand jaywalkers over a recent twelve-month period. In cases of more serious violations the penalties are exceptionally severe. A provision of Singapore's anti-drug campaign calls for drug traffickers caught in possession of specified quantities of illegal drugs to be given a mandatory death penalty.

A further instrument of political socialization is the National Service. All young men are obliged to undergo two years of full-time military training followed by periodic refresher courses in the reserves. The government views this program, instituted in 1967 by the Ministry of Defense, as an important opportunity to instill values of nationalism and discipline in young adults.

The building of a national ideology in Singapore took a dramatic turn in the 1980's. In recognition of the close relationship between liberal and critical political ideas and English-medium education and exposure, the deputy prime minister and education minister Goh Keng Swee announced in 1982 that Confucian ethics would be offered to secondary school students as a moral education option. The syllabus and text to be used in the new program were developed by the Institute of East Asian Philosophies of the National University of Singapore. Central to the new program was a stress on the "core values" of Confucian thought, including subordination of self to society, social discipline, and loyalty.

The new stress on Confucian piety acquired a broader significance when Lee Kuan Yew urged that these core values be systematically encouraged in schools and that all sectors of society, including Malays and Indians, submit their views on the proposed ideology to the government. The importance of such values was underscored by Lee's son, Lee Hsien Loong, minister of trade and industry. Unless Singaporeans paid greater heed to their Asian cultural roots, he said, "within one generation, or at most two, the spirit of Singapore will dissolve, and the nation will be no more."

Lee Kuan Yew has also proposed a change in language policy. Singapore's constitution recognizes four official languages: Malay, English, Mandarin, and Tamil. In practice English is the language of elite political and commercial life, while Malay and Chinese dialects are used in local family and business affairs. Under

Singapore's long-standing policy of multilingualism, students received bilingual education in English and a second language, often a Chinese dialect. The new policy prescribes Mandarin as the second language, in order both to enhance national identity, and, more important, to provide a more sound basis for the propagation of Confucian morality.

As part of his effort to revitalize Confucian Chinese culture, Lee supported the founding of the Singapore Federation of Chinese Clan Associations in 1986. His endorsement marked a clear reversal of his earlier efforts to destroy the Chinese foundations of leftist opposition in Singapore. While the Chinese, who comprise roughly 76% of the population, have offered little resistance to the new language policy, Malays and Indians have raised pointed questions about their future role in a more Chinese Singapore.

The PAP has attempted further social engineering in education, family relations, and population planning. Rigorous educational streaming of primary school students into vocational and academic tracks and strict quotas for the number of students allowed to major in particular subjects at the university level are intended to match educational qualifications with anticipated job openings. A general priority on technical and vocational education has been associated with a highly restrictive university entry policy. Only 12% of Singapore's eligible age group obtains a tertiary education, as opposed to 30% in Japan and 32% in South Korea.

In order to encourage greater responsibility on the part of young adults for their older and retired parents and thus to avoid the need for state welfare support for the elderly in an aging population, the PAP has promoted the "three-tier family" through preferential public housing allocation and tax incentives for young couples who support aging parents living with them in the same household.

Singapore's Family Planning Board provides a final example of developmental social engineering. This board conducted a highly effective campaign to reduce birth rates during the 1970's. In addition to a continuing media barrage of messages extolling the benefits of the small family, the government employed a stringent system of social disincentives. Maternity hospital costs were increased for third and fourth births, and third children were to be given reduced priority in school selection. The family planning program was so successful that officials began to be concerned that birth rates had fallen too low; by 1975 birth rates had reached replacement levels, leading to fears of future labor shortages and an aging population. By the early 1980's Singapore's fertility rate was the lowest in Asia, at 1.44 births per woman of childbearing age. An entirely new policy launched in 1983 encouraged more births with incentives such as a huge income tax deduction of US$ 10,650 for the third child (this was extended to the fourth child starting in 1990), and subsidies for child care, and priority in allocation of public housing units for couples with more than two children. In 1988, one year after the final disbanding of the Family Planning Board, an official announcement noted with some relief that fertility rates had risen to 1.9 children per woman.

Far more controversial was a new selective pro-natalist program which some observers regarded as a modern brand of eugenics. The government launched a campaign encouraging female college graduates to marry and have children; lower-income, less well-educated women were encouraged with cash bonuses of US$ 5,300 to be sterilized after the birth of a second child. The most bizarre element in the pro-natalist program was the establishment of a Social Development Unit to promote increased fertility among better-educated women by offering college graduates matchmaking services (including boat cruises and dances) in order to encourage earlier marriage. Prime Minister Lee justified the new policy by arguing that more affluent families were better able to provide for the educational and other developmental needs of three or four children than were poorer families, and that relatively higher fertility among lower-class families would inevitably lead to an inferior and less well-educated Singaporean population.

The pro-natalist program has been controversial. One point of opposition is that Malays and Indians tend to have lower income and education, but higher fertility rates than Chinese, and that the Chinese-dominated PAP might in fact be attempting to maintain Chinese numerical dominance in Singapore. This suspicion has been intensified by recent government efforts to attract up to one hundred thousand immigrants from Hong Kong, a predominantly Chinese city.

The rationale—and consequence—of such deep political and moral intrusion in social life is threefold. It coercively undercuts potential opposition to PAP rule. It builds positive public support for government policy through preemptive grassroots organization and ideological persuasion. Finally, it provides the social basis for a "developmental state" exempted from public debate, whose political autonomy enables it to impose its technocratic vision in shaping development policy and to implement such policy quickly and decisively in response to changing circumstances. In 1984 Lee Kuan Yew articulated his view of the relationship between social regulation and economic development:

> I say without the slightest remorse that that we wouldn't be here, would not have made the economic progress, if we had not intervened on very personal matters...who your neighbor is, how you live, the noise you make, how you spit (or where you spit), or what language you use.... It was fundamental social and cultural changes that brought us here.

Singapore's stern and puritanical regime of Confucian developmental paternalism thus combines strict political and moral regulation, state-led economic growth, and provision for social and economic welfare. On the one hand it exhibits a manifest concern for social well-being. On the other, however, it demands loyalty, compliance, and strict moral rectitude. The PAP exacts a price for the high standard of living it has been able to provide.

Future Prospects

Few observers, including even Singapore's minuscule organized opposition, would slight the tremendous economic and welfare gains that Singapore has achieved during the past thirty years of PAP rule. The major questions now posed by Singapore's development relate primarily to the continuation of the economic and political structures that propelled the republic so successfully through its earlier stages of development; Singapore's political structures and policies have become increasingly anachronistic and are unlikely to be effective in directing growth in the 1990's and beyond. In particular, analysts are questioning the developmental dead end of Singapore's continued reliance on low-cost export production; the growing clumsiness of the republic's developmental government in a complex modern economy; the long-term consequences of Singapore's marginalization of domestic capital in favor of foreign and state enterprise; and the declining efficacy and legitimacy of strict political regulation and control, especially in the context of Lee Kuan Yew's retirement in 1990.

The PAP has sought to discourage further investment in labor-intensive production, favoring higher-value-added manufacturing and service activities, but in the absence of successful economic restructuring the government has had to revert continually to its older strategy of wage restraint, tax reduction, and other cost containment policies. This dilemma becomes ever more problematic, both politically and economically, as labor shortages and upward wage pressures intensify the need for a rapid transition. The political dimensions of this problem are evidenced by growing demands for large pay increases by workers in electronics and other labor-intensive sectors after several years of union-supported wage restraint.

The developmental rationale for extensive government economic intervention is by no means as clear as it used to be. The recession of 1985–86 led to official recognition that wage regulation, a huge public enterprise sector, and other forms of government intervention had become blunt and ineffective instruments of development policy in an increasingly complex economy. Official policy now supports greater reliance on market forces, a gradual privatization of government enterprise, and more support for domestic private businesses.

Many economic sectors have long been dominated by either state or foreign enterprise. While domestic manufacturing entrepreneurship has largely atrophied, however, it has become increasingly apparent that many foreign firms are unwilling instruments of economic restructuring, often preferring to relocate to other cheap-labor sites instead of investing in new technology and higher-value activities in Singapore. It is uncertain whether local firms will be able to respond to new government incentives to participate more vigorously in Singapore's economic transformation. If they cannot, the PAP is unlikely to reduce the island's dependence on foreign capital or to dismantle a state enterprise sector which has in part functioned to counterbalance foreign investment.

To a new generation of young, well-educated, and economically secure Singaporeans, memories of unemployment and poverty no longer legitimate a continuing subordination of personal independence to economic growth. More and more young adults are migrating abroad to escape the stifling social atmosphere of Lee Kuan Yew's developmental hothouse. In 1988, 4,700 people emigrated from Singapore, most of them young and well educated. The most common reasons they cited for leaving were the pressure of work, competition, and political restrictions and regulations.

Further questions arise in connection with Lee's retirement. Under Lee's leadership top government positions have been filled by extremely bright and well-trained technocrats, many of whom lack the personal charisma or political savvy of the prime minister. It is questionable whether electoral support for the PAP can be maintained under the new prime minister, Goh Chok Tong. In keeping with his own uncertainty about Singapore's future, Lee himself will not disappear from Singapore's political landscape after retirement. Rather, he will stay on as a senior cabinet adviser and as head of the ruling party. There is even talk of his assuming the presidency under new legislation which substantially strengthens the president's oversight of the national budget and key government appointments. Lee is apparently unwilling to relinquish his guardianship of the miracle republic he has built. He was quoted in a pre-retirement interview as saying, "Even from my sickbed, even if you are going to lower me in my grave and I feel something is going wrong, I'll get up."

Hong Kong:
Diminishing Laissez-Faire

John P. Burns

Like Asia's other minidragons, during the past thirty years the British Crown colony of Hong Kong has experienced high rates of export-led growth based on labor-intensive manufacturing. Three major themes run through the story of these achievements. The first is the scope and role of the state. From the beginning British colonial authorities conceived of the state in minimalist terms. The colony of Hong Kong was simply to serve as a base for trade between China and the West. Consequently in the years that followed the state left economic development largely in the hands of private entrepreneurs, while a small cadre of civil officials managed state affairs with particular attention to issues of domestic stability and international security. A correlate of this minimalist state was a laissez-faire policy regarding state intervention in the economy.

This minimalist, non-interventionist colonial state in Hong Kong has often been contrasted with the situation in some of the other minidragons where large state bureaucracies have routinely intervened in financial and trade matters by setting protective tariffs or managing investment. However, such a contrast can be overdone. The government has consistently been committed to the provision of the political stability necessary for economic growth. Moreover, during the 1960's and 1970's, as the structure of the economy changed from manufacturing to the provision of financial services, direct and indirect state intervention has intensified and the size and importance of government has grown. While clearly not as intrusive as the state in the other minidragons, the British colonial government has been an important—and growing—factor in accounting for Hong Kong's economic miracle.

John P. Burns teaches political science at the University of Hong Kong. He has written widely in the area of Chinese politics with a particular focus on participation and political organization. His books include *Political Participation in Rural China* and *The Hong Kong Civil Service*. He has recently published a study of staffing in the Chinese bureaucracy entitled *The Chinese Communist Party's Nomenklatura System*.

Notes for this chapter can be found on pages 187–192

The second theme is the key role played in economic development by an indigenous business elite. Hong Kong's business elite has initiated and facilitated economic development, performing many of the same functions of more interventionist states in the other newly-industrializing nations. Local banks in particular have guided investment strategies to promote economic growth. Finally, relative political stability has contributed significantly to Hong Kong's economic success. Until recently the government has achieved stability either by co-opting its critics or by accommodating them through policy changes. In the 1980's, however, the government has frustrated the demands of Hong Kong's rapidly rising middle class, thus undermining political stability. Uncertainty about Hong Kong's future after 1997 has also been destabilizing. These factors are likely to depress future economic growth in the territory.

In this chapter we begin with an examination of the nature of British colonialism in Hong Kong. Then we look at Hong Kong's postwar economic development, highlighting structural changes in the economy. We consider the reasons for Hong Kong's economic success, examining in particular the interaction between local business leaders and the state in fostering economic growth. Finally, we discuss critical political issues, including the colony's stability and the impact of the planned transition to Chinese rule in 1997.

British Colonialism in Hong Kong

Hong Kong today is a small, highly urbanized city-state with neither an agricultural sector nor natural resources apart from an excellent harbor. In 1990 Hong Kong's 5.8 million people occupied 1,073 square kilometers, a land area about the size of Rhode Island. The territory is made up of Hong Kong island, where the financial center is located; Kowloon peninsula, a densely populated residential and commercial area across the harbor from Hong Kong Island; and the New Territories, a district which includes 235 nearby islands and makes up 92% of the area of Hong Kong, and which is now the site of Hong Kong's booming light industry and high-rise new towns. Located on China's southern coast on the Pearl River delta, Hong Kong lies contiguous to Guangdong province, with which it shares deep family, cultural, economic, and (especially) linguistic ties. Most of Hong Kong's population is Cantonese speaking; more than 40% are themselves immigrants from China.

In pre-colonial times Hong Kong was ruled by officials of imperial China as part of Guangdong province. During the nineteenth century the territory that now makes up Hong Kong was acquired by Great Britain in three stages, principally as a base for trade. In 1842, as part of the settlement of the First Opium War, Great Britain obtained Hong Kong island. Nearly twenty years later, after a military defeat in the Second Opium War, China ceded Kowloon peninsula, giving the British control over both sides of an excellent harbor. After China's defeat in the 1895 Sino-Japanese War, the Chinese government granted concessions to France, Germany, and Russia. In 1898 Great Britain took advantage of China's weakness to persuade the Chinese government to sign a ninety-nine-year lease on the New Territories.

Apart from occasional labor unrest such as the seamen's strike of 1922, Hong Kong was little affected by China's internal political conflicts during the early twentieth century. In 1941, however, the Japanese army invaded Hong Kong, imprisoned the British authorities, and virtually destroyed the local economy. British rule was not restored until 1945. In the decades that followed, despite the waves of decolonialization, it remained a British Crown Colony. The approaching expiration of the lease on the economically vital New Territories on June 30, 1997, prompted Great Britain in 1982 to enter into negotiations with the People's Republic of China (PRC) to determine the future of Hong Kong. Two years later the countries signed an agreement providing for the transfer of sovereignty over Hong Kong to the PRC on July 1, 1997.

When the British arrived on Hong Kong island, they found a few thousand indigenous inhabitants, mostly fishermen, scattered in some twenty villages. Colonial administrators therefore did not have to contend with powerful, entrenched local interests; they had a relatively free hand. In keeping with Great Britain's standard colonial practice, the administration in Hong Kong comprised a small number of civilian officials whose charge was simply to maintain a minimal state.

Although Hong Kong has served as a base for the British garrison in East Asia, historically its principal function has been as a base for trade. The colony served as an important trade link between China and the West during the late nineteenth century. In 1890, for example, 55% of China's imports and 37% of its exports passed through the territory. By 1900 these figures had fallen to 42% and 40% respectively, as other ports developed on the China coast. During these years China's largest foreign trade partner was the British empire, although Germany, France, Russia, and Japan were growing competitors. China dominated Hong Kong's foreign trade during the early and mid-twentieth century; from 1931 to 1938, 45% to 59% of Hong Kong's exports and 27% to 38% of its imports involved trade with China. Much of this was *entrepot* trade.

With this limited view of the territory's usefulness, the British government kept the activities of its administration in Hong Kong to a minimum. The colonial government assumed responsibility for law and order; the administration of justice; the provision (eventually) of a few essential services such as sanitation; and the raising of revenue to pay for these services, an activity that involved the government in land management. Both the British authorities in London and the traders attracted to Hong Kong were interested in a minimal colonial state that delivered value for money.

British colonial policy in Hong Kong can best be described as conditional *laissez-faire* with stability as its overriding concern. The authorities were uninterested in propagating the official ideologies such as Confucianism that have characterized indigenous East Asian regimes. Indeed, according to two prominent students of British policy, traditional Chinese values have "drastically weakened" in the territory precisely because colonial authorities have maintained such a hands-off policy, refusing to act as "powerful custodians to uphold and enforce Confucian morality and virtues."

Through most of its colonial history the government in Hong Kong has been authoritarian. In a formula unchanged from the 1890's until the mid-1960's, political power was centralized in the colonial civil service, which permitted small numbers of businessmen to address it through the appointed Legislative and Executive Councils but excluded everyone else. Only when the stability of the colony was threatened did the state reluctantly agree to permit business elites some representation in the decision-making process. However, for the ordinary people in Hong Kong, the state remained as "faceless...cold, impersonal, unconcerned with human feelings, hidebound and aloof."

Hong Kong's colonial status continues to have an impact on its political development. Predictably, colonial authorities have not encouraged the development of political parties, democratic institutions, mass-based political movements, or political activism in the territory. Such moves might have threatened political stability. With the agreement to turn Hong Kong over to the PRC in 1997, however, a unique set of decolonialization arrangements has been put in place. Rather than granting independence to the territory as it has with its other colonies, Great Britain has instead agreed to hand Hong Kong over to another country. Unlike many colonial societies, Hong Kong has thus never undergone a struggle for independence during which legitimate, credible, and indigenous leaders and political movements could emerge. Without this opportunity to forge a national consensus on either economic policy or a legitimate government to implement it, Hong Kong faces an uncertain political future after 1997.

Economic Development

External Shocks

When Great Britain regained control of Hong Kong from Japan at the end of the Second World War, it took over "a run-down, war-damaged, pre-industrial society with no very evident future." Gradually, however, the territory attempted to resume its role in the *entrepot* trade between China and the West.

During the next few years Hong Kong's economy was rocked by two international events. First, the civil war in China encouraged mainland-based capitalists to step up their search for a safe haven from both the violence and growing Nationalist government controls of the economy; during the late 1940's, many mainland Chinese were attracted to Hong Kong. As early as 1947 exiled Shanghainese textile owners established the first spinning mill in the colony. An Anglo-Chinese group set up the first spinning and weaving mill a year later. From 1947 to 1951 the number of spindles installed in Hong Kong rose from 6,000 to 180,000. The role of Shanghainese capital and entrepreneurs in the subsequent industrialization of Hong Kong cannot be overestimated.

The civil war in China also drove huge numbers of refugees to flee to Hong Kong. From a wartime low of 600,000, Hong Kong's population had grown to 1.6 million by 1948. In 1949 and 1950 alone an estimated 330,000 immigrants arrived from the mainland—indeed, at one point in 1949, 10,000 refugees were arriving in Hong Kong every week. These and subsequent waves of immigrants from the PRC in the 1950's provided a pool of cheap, unorganized labor for Hong Kong.

The civil war disrupted trading relationships by rendering Hong Kong's traditional markets in China uncertain. With the establishment of a relatively stable government in the PRC, however, prospects for Hong Kong to resume its *entrepot* role improved. Hong Kong's merchants resumed their purchases of Chinese raw materials (bristles, seeds, raw silk, animal and vegetable oils, and so forth) and consumer goods (tea, pottery, and handicrafts) for sale in Europe and North America. And they imported industrial raw materials and finished producers' and consumer goods from the West and Japan for sale in China. Hong Kong's reliance on trade was nearly absolute. By the early 1950's there had been so little industrialization that only 10% of Hong Kong's exports were produced locally, and only 60,000 to 70,000 people were employed in manufacturing.

The second external shock to Hong Kong's economy was the Korean War in June 1950. Part of Britain's response to the war, undertaken in cooperation with the United States, was an embargo on trade with China. As a British colony Hong Kong was directly involved—and with devastating economic consequences. The embargo severely curtailed both the PRC's importation of "strategic goods" and its re-exports through Hong Kong. The territory's exports to the PRC fell from HK$ 1.6 billion in 1952 to HK$ 520 million a year later, dwindling to HK$ 136 million in 1956.

Political developments in the PRC and in East Asia therefore pushed the business community in Hong Kong straight into a strategy of manufacturing for export. Unlike the other minidragons, Hong Kong did not go through a period of import substituting industrialization (ISI). The small size of Hong Kong's domestic market provided local manufacturers with a strong incentive to concentrate on exports from the beginning. The colony certainly benefited indirectly, though, from the import substitution practices that had nurtured Shanghai capitalists, especially during the 1920's and 1930's. Some commentators have argued that Hong Kong actually underwent "a period of disguised [import substitution] on the mainland. It was under sheltered conditions that the entrepreneurial capabilities of the Shanghai capitalists had developed—not to mention their fixed capital and plant, some of which ultimately found its way to Hong Kong."

Growth of the Economy

Although the Hong Kong economy has experienced "hyper-growth," especially in the early 1960's and from 1969 to 1982, the rate of growth has varied widely. These variations can be explained by domestic and external political and economic factors.

Throughout the 1950's Hong Kong experienced relatively high rates of growth as it developed its manufacturing capacity. According to World Bank estimates, average annual gross domestic product (GDP) grew by about 9.2% during the decade. Only after 1960, however, when its GDP reached HK$ 6 billion, did Hong Kong begin to achieve consistent annual growth rates of more than 10%. Even then there were lean times; a banking crisis in 1965 and the riots of 1966–67 resulted in poor economic performance during those years. Hong Kong's GDP grew from HK$ 15.6 billion in 1968 to HK$ 39 billion in 1973; this period of rapid growth lasted until 1982, interrupted only by a world economic recession in 1974–75. Political and economic factors combined to drive the rate of growth down in 1982–83; in 1984–85, the economy actually declined. These years were influenced by a second oil crisis in 1982 and by the near collapse of the Sino-British negotiations on the future of Hong Kong in 1983.

Conflict in the negotiations created a political crisis in 1983 that also precipitated a steep slide in the value of the Hong Kong dollar, which fell by 15% in two days during September of that year to hit a historic low of US$ 1 to HK$ 9.6. The crisis of confidence in the colony's political future led to the collapse of the unquestionably inflated local real estate market and induced a run on local banks. A total breakdown of the financial system in 1983 was averted only by the government's takeover of the Hang Lung Bank, its assistance to the Sun Hung Kai Bank, and a currency stabilization program pegging the Hong Kong dollar to the U.S. dollar at a rate of 1:7.8. Economic recovery was aided not only by the 1984 agreement between Britain and the PRC on the future of Hong Kong, but by the expansion of the American economy, Hong Kong's largest export market. Rates of growth fell once again from 1987 to 1989, however. GDP increased from HK$ 229.4 billion to HK$ 252.1 billion during that period, increasing 7.2% in 1987–88 and 2.5% in 1988–89. Reduced demand in the United States for Hong Kong products and the austerity measures taken in 1988 in the PRC to cool its economy and recentralize economic control contributed to this decline.

Structural Change

During the 1950's, reacting to the restrictions placed on *entrepot* trade by the embargo on the PRC, Hong Kong entrepreneurs turned their attention to manufacturing. From 1950 to mid-1956 the number of registered factories increased by nearly 83% to 3,200, while the number of workers employed in manufacturing increased by almost 60% to 145,000. Most of these workers were employed in small firms producing textiles and metal products. During the 1960's, not surprisingly, the contribution of manufacturing to total GDP rose as well, increasing from 23.6% in 1961 to 30.8% in 1970. In the peak year of 1971 more than 47% of Hong Kong's working population was employed in manufacturing, which at the time was the territory's largest employer.

Textile production has dominated manufacturing in Hong Kong since the 1950's. In 1955 more than 28% of all laborers in manufacturing were employed in textile production, most of it concentrated in a few large operations such as Hong Kong Spinners, Wyler Textiles, and South Sea Textile Manufacturing, all firms with more than a thousand employees, and in a dozen or so smaller operations. In recent years, however, textiles have lost their dominant role in Hong Kong; from 1973 to 1987 textile production's share of manufacturing output fell from 27% to 17%, its share of manufacturing employment from 21% to 14%. Many small textile manufacturers have gone out of business, leaving a few major players which produce both textiles and garments: Winsor Industrial, Jian Sin Mee Holdings, Nan Fung Textiles, and Yangtzekiang Garments. Many manufacturers have shifted from textiles into garment and finished-clothing production in recent years. From 1973 to 1987 clothing production's share of manufacturing output rose from 20% to 24%, its share of manufacturing employment from 26% to 29%.

In addition to textiles and garments, Hong Kong's manufacturers have produced electrical appliances and, more recently, watches and clocks. From 1973 to 1987 the share of manufacturing output in these two sectors has increased from

9% to 15% and 1% to 3% respectively. In the mid-1980's Conic Investments, Wong's Industrial Holdings, and Chuang's Holdings were major players in the electronics sectors, while Stelux Holdings was a major producer of watches and clocks.

Beginning in the early 1970's Hong Kong's economy underwent a basic structural change: manufacturing lost its dominant position to the financial services sector. In decline since 1972, the contribution of manufacturing to GDP was only 20.4% of the total in 1988. Although it continues to be the territory's largest employer, by 1989 manufacturing employed only about 30% of the work force. Over the same period financial services—banking, investment services, insurance, real estate, and provision of business services to foreign companies—have grown, overtaking manufacturing as a proportion of GDP for the first time in 1980. Since then the size of the financial sector has varied considerably, falling to 16% of GDP in 1984, a drop that reflected the collapse of the property market a year earlier. After 1984, however, it rose steadily, contributing 19% of GDP in 1988. The most prominent players in the financial service sector include the Hong Kong and Shanghai Banking Corporation (hereafter Hong Kong Bank) as well as real estate and investment companies such as Hong Kong Land, Cheung Kong Holdings, and New World Development Corporation.

The relative decline of manufacturing and growth of financial services can be explained by several factors. First, because Hong Kong's manufacturing is highly concentrated on a few end products that are in turn overly dependent on the American market, the industry has been adversely affected by protectionist pressures in the United States. Hong Kong's manufacturing has focused on garments and textiles, electronics, plastics, and, more recently, watches and clocks. In 1989 these few products accounted for 66% of Hong Kong's total manufacturing and 71% of its total exports. These items have been exported mostly to the United States. Every year from 1968 to 1988 between 33% and 44% of Hong Kong's total domestic exports were destined for the American market.

The United States has imposed increasingly tight restrictions on the importation of garments and textiles since 1961, first under the auspices of the General Agreement on Tariffs and Trade (GATT) and from 1974 under the Multi-Fiber Arrangement (MFA). Great Britain and the European Economic Community (EEC) have imposed similar restrictions. As a consequence the growth of textile and garment manufacture in Hong Kong has slowed, although manufacturers have demonstrated considerable flexibility by switching production to goods made of silk and vegetable fibers not covered by quota restrictions.

Another reason for the recent decline in manufacturing is that Hong Kong businessmen have moved some of their production to the PRC's special economic zones to take advantages of cheaper land and labor. A 1987 survey found that among small- and medium-sized factories in Hong Kong, the dominant group in local manufacturing, 19% had established out-processing factories in the Pearl River delta, where labor costs are only about one-third those in Hong Kong. Indeed, by 1989 Hong Kong industries, including Success Shoes, Jianli Handbags, Superjack Electric Motors, and Hangli and Luen Fat Toy Manufacturers, were employing an estimated 2.5 million workers across the border. Shifting production to the PRC has clearly contributed to the declining share of manufacturing in the GDP.

The PRC has also played a major role in the development of a financial services industry in Hong Kong as the territory has rushed to provide financial services to the newly reopened China trade. The post-1979 economic reforms in the PRC, in particular the "open door policy," have produced a dramatic increase in trade between the two countries. In less than a decade after the reforms were instituted, total exports to the PRC from Hong Kong, largely electrical appliances and semi-finished electronic products, grew from HK$ 4.6 billion to HK$ 146.8 billion; imports from the PRC of such items as food and coal increased from nearly HK$ 22 billion to almost HK$ 200 billion. At the same time Hong Kong businesses have been the largest foreign investors in the PRC, accounting for 65% of direct foreign investment from 1976 to 1986. To facilitate this vastly increased trade and Hong Kong investment in the mainland, a strong financial services sector has emerged in Hong Kong. Because of its close proximity to the PRC and its lack of foreign exchange controls, Hong Kong has eclipsed Singapore in the provision of financial services to businesses trading in East Asia.

Hong Kong's Economic Success

A number of factors have contributed to Hong Kong's exceptionally strong economic performance. As we have seen, the civil war in China and the Korean War pushed the colony's entrepreneurs into export-oriented manufacturing at an early stage of its economic development. Hong Kong also benefited from an expanding world economy, particularly from the economic boom in the United States during the 1960's and 1970's, which enabled Hong Kong manufacturers to succeed with an export strategy. In addition to these factors, three characteristics of Hong Kong were critical: a strong, adaptable and relatively unified local business elite; an industrial work force that was hardworking and frugal but organizationally weak; and a generally stable political environment that valued free enterprise.

Foreign capital has played an important role in Hong Kong's economic development by providing new technology, management skills, and investment in new industries, but it has not dominated the economy as it has in Singapore. Nor

Hong Kong

Hong Kong harbor. Now as in the past this sheltered, natural deep-water harbor is Hong Kong's most important natural resource.

One of the few rural areas in the New Territories.

A fishing village on Peng Chau island.

Despite a public housing program that houses nearly half of the population, quality and availability of living accommodations are often poor.

Recently built high-rise housing in Shatin, a new town development reclaimed from the shallow bay at Tide Cove.

Landmark of the Causeway Bay district, this white pagoda in now-public Tiger Balm Garden was built by Aw Boon Haw, who made a fortune from the sale of "tiger balm."

A Hong Kong fruit and vegetable market.

Hong Kong business women keep in touch with the office.

Worshippers at Wong Tai Sin Temple light incense sticks and pray for fulfillment of their wishes.

The Hong Kong Correctional
Services march in full regalia.

View of Hong Kong's Central
District from Victoria Peak. Across
the bay lies Kowloon.

A busy street in the Chinese district of Kowloon.

Hong Kong women cutting fabric in a clothing factory.

School children busily at work on their assignments.

Stacks of just-completed blue jeans ready for packaging and shipment.

Modern skyscrapers are still built with use of bamboo scaffolding.

Most of Hong Kong's thousands of boats are homes or working vessels.

Land reclamation makes space for more construction

A jumbo jet taking off from busy Kai Tak Airport, which extends into Kowloon Bay.

A shoemaker's workshop in Hong Kong.

Kwai Chung container terminal
has the highest throughput of
containers of any port in the
world.

Neon signs light up the night in
Hong Kong.

Hong Kong and Shanghai
Banking Corporation, established
in 1865 and now one of the ten
largest banks in Asia.

The Hong Kong Stock Exchange is a symbol of Hong Kong's relatively open economy.

Gardens surround Kam Tin walled village in the New Territories.

Aberdeen Harbor, jammed with fishing junks.

A long queue in front of the American Consulate, seeking the opportunity to leave Hong Kong.

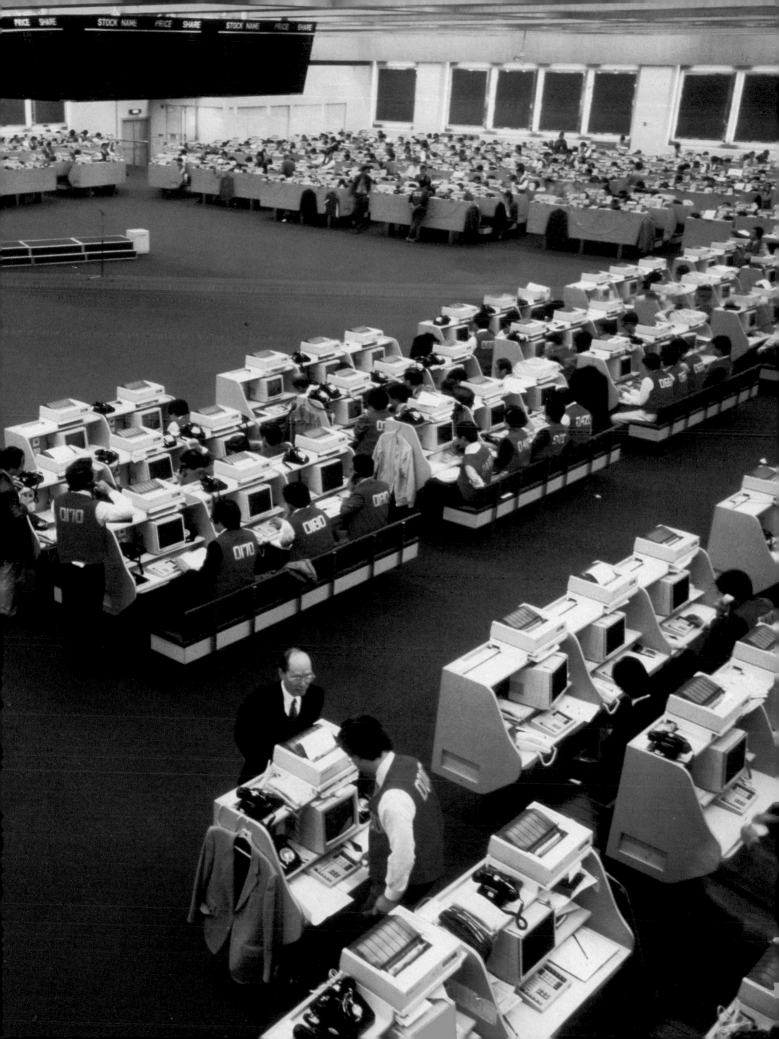

A principal road link with China
at Lok Ma Chau nears completion.

A huge rally in Hong Kong
protests killings and arrests of
students in the PRC.

Hong Kong citizens protest
limitations on availability of
British citizenship.

has the state played a direct or expansive role in Hong Kong's economic growth. Instead an indigenous business elite has directed the territory's economic development. As one study points out, private firms such as Jardine Matheson and the Hong Kong Bank have "performed some of the functions taken on by the state in [South Korea, Taiwan, and Singapore], including financing of infrastructure and investment in and promotion of smaller enterprises."

The role of local commercial banks, especially the Hong Kong Bank, in the territory's early industrialization was especially crucial. Most of the industrialists who fled from the mainland to Hong Kong arrived with no collateral; the commercial banks responded by abandoning their traditional role as short-term lenders, providing the long-term financing that these entrepreneurs needed. One commentator has noted that without this flexible response by the banks, "there would never have been a successful Industrial Revolution in Hong Kong."

Since the late nineteenth century Hong Kong's bankers have regulated competition among themselves by gentlemen's agreements, fixing the prices of a wide range of banking services, including exchange rates. Reduced competition helped to promote the relative stability that Hong Kong enjoyed until the 1970's. In the 1980's, however, when financial stability was undermined by cutthroat competition from newly established deposit-taking corporations, these informal arrangements were replaced by statutory controls which set up the Hong Kong Association of Banks, the rules and regulations of which were binding on its members. The Hong Kong Bank, established in 1865 and now one of the ten largest banks in Asia, has played a leading role in these activities because of its long history, its size, and the semi-official role assigned to it by the government. Consistent with its minimalist approach to economic management, the colonial government never established a central bank in Hong Kong. Instead it assigned some central banking functions to various government departments and others to the Hong Kong Bank (which, for example, is one of two banks that issues the territory's bank notes).

Hong Kong's business elite has been comparatively cohesive and concentrated. A relatively small group of bankers has been linked to strategic business and government elites through interlocking company directorships; memberships in such bodies as the Board of Education and the Labour, Transport, and Port Advisory Committees; participation in business associations like the Chamber of Commerce; and informal interaction. At the height of the boom in manufacturing in 1970, for example, the unofficial membership in the Executive and Legislative Councils, bodies set up to advise the colonial governor on policy, included the chairman and three directors of the Hong Kong Bank. These directors, in turn, were concurrently directors of major trading houses such as Hutchison, Wheelock Marden, Swire, and

Jardine Matheson, directors of major public utilities, and members of strategic business associations such as the chambers of commerce. This pattern of a highly concentrated business elite working closely with government to develop the economy continued throughout the 1970's and 1980's. There is no question that Hong Kong's business leaders and government officials share a belief in the primacy of private enterprise.

Hong Kong owes its economic success as much to its hardworking and frugal industrial work force as it does to their bosses. Immigrants from the mainland and the indigenous population alike practice what one specialist on Hong Kong, Lau Siu-kai, calls "utilitarianistic familism." The people of Hong Kong have tended to place the interests of the family group first, and among family interests, material concerns have received top priority. In fact, Lau concludes, "material values reign supreme in Hong Kong." Immigrants make up a very large proportion of the population, and Lau traces their materialistic orientation to the self-selecting process by which the colony tended to attract those who sought to take advantage of Hong Kong's relatively open society to achieve material advancement. Most immigrants came from neighboring Guangdong province, which was already heavily commercialized. Lau notes, too, that "the lack of traditional Chinese moral constraints on uninhibited efforts at material gain in a migrant society such as Hong Kong sets free the rampant and rapacious desire for material advancement." Another reason for the pursuit of material success is that Hong Kong's colonial status has meant that the top positions in government are reserved for expatriates. With upward mobility blocked in the political arena, many people in Hong Kong have undoubtedly turned to economic mobility to gain prestige and status.

Hong Kong's hardworking industrial labor force has accepted relatively low wages, long hours and often poor working conditions. They were not protected by minimum wage laws, comprehensive workers' compensation, or a central provident scheme. In part these conditions were the product of the weakness of the labor movement in Hong Kong, a weakness which can be traced to several characteristics of the employment structure in the territory.

For forty years employers in Hong Kong have been able to draw on a huge pool of immigrant labor replenished periodically by new arrivals, mostly from neighboring Guangdong and Fujian provinces. During the period of "open door" economic reforms and relaxed border controls in the PRC from 1978 to 1981, half a million legal and illegal immigrants arrived in the territory. Despite an attempt in 1981 to implement stringent controls on immigration from the PRC, illegal immigrants have arrived in large numbers to take up insecure employment in Hong Kong. Their tenuous position makes them poor prospects for labor organizing.

Another factor contributing to a politically weak work force is that manufacturing in Hong Kong is dominated by small and medium-sized enterprises. In 1971, 60% of manufacturing businesses in Hong Kong employed fewer than two hundred workers; by 1984 the figure had grown to 70%. Small businesses in Hong Kong tend to be family businesses with paternalistic employment practices. Neither the small size nor the family orientation of manufacturing enterprises in Hong Kong provides fertile ground for the development of strong unions.

Hong Kong's labor-intensive light manufacturing has tended to attract young female workers in large numbers. Among the manufacturing labor force the proportion of female workers has steadily increased from 33% in 1961 to 46% in 1986. These young women have contributed to higher turnover rates by working for short periods and leaving their jobs to get married or rear families. Stable labor forces are more likely to spawn strong labor movements.

Although the colonial state has recognized the right of workers in Hong Kong to join trade unions, only about 20% of the labor force has done so. The government has legally regulated union activity: unions must register with the government, must ensure that trade disputes follow certain rules (they may not "restrain trade," for example), and may not federate across industries or occupations. Since the late 1970's, however, the government has improved the regulation of industrial safety and expanded the rights of workers to severance pay, holidays, and compulsory rest days. One commentator in 1980 termed the remaining official restrictions on labor "insubstantial."

The prohibition on amalgamations has, however, contributed to the fragmentation of the trade union movement in Hong Kong. In 1977 over half of the 327 registered trade unions in the territory had 250 members or less, while nearly 40% had fifty members or less. Political divisions have also fragmented the union movement, which for most of the past forty years has been divided into pro-communist, pro-nationalist, and neutral camps. During the 1980's and especially after the signing of the Sino-British agreement, membership in the pro-nationalist unions has declined, refocusing union conflict on the split between independent and pro-communist organizations. Conflict between employers and the pro-communist unions has been muted, however, by the PRC's insistence that these unions promote stability in the territory.

Government and the Economy

Since the late 1940's, the state has not played the strong, directive role in Hong Kong's economic development that it has in the other minidragons, and this is reflected in the structure of the government. Hong Kong is a free port, has no exchange controls, does not protect industry, has few restrictions on private ownership, has virtually no public enterprise, and has placed public utilities and most public transport in the hands of private companies. The principle explanation for this situation is the fact that the colony bypassed a period of ISI, a strategy that requires direct state intervention to erect tariff barriers and to direct investment toward high-priority infant industries. As a result, two prominent commentators on Hong Kong have argued that "Hong Kong's economy is undoubtedly the most open and its government the least interventionist in the world." Such a contention is supported by an official statement in 1973 which described the role of the government as follows:

> Hong Kong is probably the only territory still completely faithful to liberal economic policies of free enterprise and free trade.... Economic planning is not a function of the government except in the very broadest sense. Apart from the provision of the infrastructure...the government's role remains one of providing a suitable framework within which commerce and industry can function efficiently and effectively with a minimum of interference.

However, the reality of Hong Kong differs significantly from these assertions. The state's role in the economy has been more extensive than is commonly realized. And it has grown in recent years.

The first manifestation of Government influence on the economy is to be found in the management of land. At the time of its establishment in the 1840's, British authorities determined that the new colony of Hong Kong should not be a drain on the Treasury, and ensured a local source of revenue by granting the colonial government ownership of virtually all the land in Hong Kong. The government in turn sold long-term leases to private citizens; proceeds from the auction of leaseholds has formed an important part of government revenue ever since. From time to time the government has used its ownership of land to assist priority industries such as textile manufacturers by selling them land by private treaty or by offering them especially favorable terms such as lower interest rates. Government decisions on the amounts of land to be sold and its zoning also have an impact on the market.

The government also exerts economic influence through control of public utilities. Although these utilities are owned privately in Hong Kong, the state maintains control over their charges and profits, and civil servants serve as directors on some utilities' boards.

The financial sector has been another important area where government influence is felt. Throughout the period of rapid industrialization, the government sought to stabilize the financial sector and ensure Hong Kong's continued attractiveness to international investors by working closely with Hong Kong's commercial banks, especially the Hong Kong Bank, in what one observer called a "distinctly symbiotic relationship." A series of crises that rocked the banking establishment during the early and mid-1960's and again in the mid-1980's revealed the government's indirect but critical involvement. In 1965 the colonial state took over and liquidated two failed banks. It also coordinated the rescue efforts undertaken by the two note-issuing banks, the Hong Kong Bank and the Standard Chartered Bank, to support several other troubled banks.

In a speech in 1977 Financial Secretary Sir Philip Haddon-Cave seemed to recognize the increasing role for government in several areas including the financial sector. He acknowledged that the colonial government was prepared to make limited interventions in foreign exchange markets; to guide and restrain the market, particularly in the financial sector; to establish a network of advisory bodies for the exchange of information between the public and private sectors; to provide services such as law and order, and defense and infrastructure such as roads and sewage systems, which could not effectively be provided by the private sector; and to establish or subsidize certain services to business which the private sector was unwilling or unable to provide.

The turbulence and political crises of the 1980's forced the government further into areas it had previously left untouched. In 1983 and 1984, in the face of an impending economic collapse caused by uncertainty over the 1997 question, official policy became more interventionist as the government moved to rescue the Hang Lung and Sun Hung Kai Banks from failure and to stabilize the Hong Kong currency by pegging it to the United States dollar. Financial Secretary John Brembridge wrote:

> *Laissez-faire* is an insulting term. What we believe in and what we practice is the theme that less government is better government. But have no doubt that we, as the Hong Kong Government, are prepared to make the decisions that a government has to in difficult circumstances.

Thus, during the 1980's, Government words and actions seemed indicative of a greater willingness to intervene in certain sectors of the economy. In all of these interventions, in the words of one observer, "the government played a crucial, albeit 'behind the scene,' role to put the deal[s] together." The government's overriding concern in doing so was to restore stability to the economy. Still, in contrast to the other minidragons, the government did not acknowledge any role in protecting industry or granting subsidies to priority industries.

However, the colonial government has been active in boosting exports and foreign investment and formulating industrial policy. Since the mid-1960's it has actively promoted exports through the state-sponsored Trade Development Council, which now has a network of overseas offices. The government's own Trade Department and Industry Department also principally serve this function. In addition the state has actively courted foreign investors and funded the Productivity Council and other bodies designed to assist industry to become more competitive. As the dangers of excessive dependence on textile exports to the United States became apparent in the mid-1970's, the government also led a major effort to study diversification strategies suggesting a greater role for government as the territory's economy has evolved from *entrepot* trade to manufacturing to the provision of financial services.

Finally, the government has intervened directly from time to time to curb perceived excesses in the market. In the early 1970's, for example, it controlled rents for domestic premises, restricted rent increases, and prevented landlords from evicting sitting tenants. The government has been a major provider of public housing since 1954; by the late 1980's almost half of the Hong Kong population were living in state-owned housing.

Since the 1950's, then, the involvement of the government in the management of the economy has been indirect but growing. Intervention has tended to occur whenever there have been crises or breakdowns in the interplay of market forces and/or the need to restore economic stability. But this economic role has not relied on the more intrusive measures (such as tariff protection, subsidies for infant industries, and central planning) that have characterized Taiwan and South Korea, countries that first adopted import-substituting strategies of industrialization.

Political Development

Hong Kong's relative political stability, especially during the 1970's, has also contributed to its economic success. As in other countries, political stability in the territory is a product of state-society relations; these relations have been strained by rapid economic development in Hong Kong. In the mid-1960's the working class demanded improved working and social conditions. In response the colonial state instituted a series of administrative reforms designed to improve government's links to local communities and to expand social welfare. Twenty years later Hong Kong's new middle class, the chief beneficiaries of economic growth, demanded a greater role in state decision-making. The state's response to this challenge has been equivocal, and the stability of the territory has been undermined as a result, endangering future economic growth in Hong Kong.

From its earliest beginnings the government of Hong Kong was typical of colonial authority in being highly centralized and authoritarian. Officially all political power resided in the governor. Appointed by the Crown, he was advised by the Executive and Legislative Councils, whose members (until very recently) he appointed himself. In practice, however, the real locus of power was in the colonial civil servants sent from London who were responsible for drafting and implementing policy.

The colonial state underwent major constitutional change on three occasions: in the 1890's, in the late 1960's and early 1970's, and in 1984. Reacting to a crisis in each case, the government attempted to win political stability either by co-opting strategic elites into the policy process or by adopting policies that would redistribute benefits to alienated groups.

During the first fifty years of Hong Kong's colonization, economic development was accompanied by the growth of a merchant class composed of both British traders and an indigenous Chinese elite. The British merchants took advantage of their representation on the Legislative Council and the Chamber of Commerce to put forward an agenda of demands—reduced taxation and limited public expenditure—which the appointed government majority on the Council was able to ignore. After several years of fruitless lobbying, the merchants' representatives petitioned London to revamp the Council by creating an elected majority. The petition was rejected, but both the British and the Hong Kong governments "recognized the need to incorporate the merchants and traditional Chinese elites into a new structure of authority." In 1896 the colonial authorities appointed the first two non-civil-servants to the Executive Council and expanded non-official representation on the Legislative Council. These arrangements, which gave considerable influence to a small business elite while excluding the rest of the community, continued until the mid-1960's.

The economic growth of the 1950's and early 1960's produced a new industrial proletariat that existed for all intents and purposes outside of the political system. These workers had no political representation whatever; their disenfranchisement, together with their primitive working conditions and subsistence standard of living, led, in the words of one commentator, "to a sense of frustration and alienation which found its outlet in anomic violence and attacks on the police."

The rhetoric of the Cultural Revolution in the PRC from 1966 to 1969 fanned nationalistic, anti-colonial flames in Hong Kong. In 1966 and 1967 the territory was rocked by a series of riots and demonstrations. The 1966 riots lasted for four days and were finally quelled by the authorities with the arrest of 427 people. The eight-month frenzy of rioting, bombing, and demonstrations in 1967 was much more serious. What began in March 1967 as a series of labor disputes involving the pro-communist Federation of Trade Unions quickly escalated into street demonstrations and riots, strikes, violence, and acts of terrorism, including bomb attacks. The major target of the violence was the colonial regime.

The violence started in May during a series of labor disputes in eight companies, all of which employed workers with strong links to the pro-communist Federation of Trade Unions. When on May 11 workers in one of these companies, the Hong Kong Artificial Flower Works, tried to break into the factory, they were arrested by the police. During the following days, rioting spread to Kowloon, buses were torched, and government offices were looted. On May 15 the PRC's Ministry of Foreign Affairs issued a statement denouncing the colonial authorities in Hong Kong and demanding an end to the violence.

In June transport workers and some government manual workers went on strike. Amid calls for a general strike, government and transport workers locked themselves in their work places; police broke in and made five hundred arrests. Local villagers attacked a police border post, there were urban demonstrations in July, and from August to September there was a rash of bomb attacks in public places. Police arrested three employees of the PRC's New China News Agency in Hong Kong for inciting the violence. When colonial authorities refused Beijing's request for their release, the office of the British charge d'affaires in Beijing was sacked. In all, fifty-one people died during the disturbances in the colony.

Most of the people in Hong Kong, repelled by the violence, supported the government in its successful effort to restore political stability. The fact that they did so fundamentally altered the nature of state-society relations leading one commentator to note that in 1967 the legitimacy of the colonial government shifted to completely new ground: the authorities could now claim to rule with the consent of the people.

To maintain its popular support the colonial state set up new consultative institutions and sought to improve social welfare. The government established city district offices that were charged to explain government policy to the public and to elicit the support of local leaders. The co-opted local leaders were invited to serve on scores of new advisory boards and committees such as street *(kaifong)* associations, mutual aid committees, and, eventually, district boards.

Throughout the 1970's the authorities also began to take a more active role in improving working conditions and providing industrial workers with social welfare. The government greatly expanded its public housing program, among other activities planning and constructing several comprehensive New Towns; funded a dramatic expansion of compulsory education through the tenth grade; upgraded social services, including medical care; and supervised the development of Hong Kong's transportation infrastructure, including container port facilities and a new subway system. None of these changes threatened the privileged position of established business elites so long as the economy continued to grow to provide a financial basis for these services.

To accommodate its new role in these areas, the state bureaucracy expanded very quickly. From 1973 to 1983 the number of civil service jobs increased by 65.5%, from 104,876 to 173,633. Government expenditure as a percentage of GDP also increased substantially during the period, rising from 11.4% in 1970–71 to a high of 19.2% in 1982–83.

The government's handling of the 1967 riots, its attempts to increase consultation, its new interest in social welfare, and the economy's rapid growth all served to increase the legitimacy of the colonial government in the eyes of the people of Hong Kong. One by-product of this new legitimacy was a relative autonomy from special interest groups. The government was able, for example, to resist demands of business groups that it reduce the cost of public utilities, extend rent control to industrial premises, provide a guaranteed market for some locally-manufactured products and, indeed, restrict the growth of the civil service.

The state's new-found legitimacy and autonomy were short lived, however. In 1982 the question mark hanging over Hong Kong's future after the expiration in 1997 of the agreement with China regarding the New Territories began to have a major impact on political and economic systems. The 1997 question emerged just as Hong Kong was developing into a regional financial center. Both of these developments left the territory vulnerable to political and economic shocks; the government was forced to intervene more directly in the economy to ensure stability at a time when it was least able to do so.

In the late 1970's and early 1980's Hong Kong business leaders, uncertain about the legal status of their investments beyond 1997, pressed the Hong Kong and British governments to resolve the problem of the 1997 lease. Britain and the PRC entered into negotiations and in 1984 signed the Sino-British joint declaration on the future of Hong Kong. This agreement has three major provisions. First, the PRC will resume sovereignty over Hong Kong on July 1, 1997, when the territory will become a special administrative region of the PRC with "a high degree of autonomy." Second, Hong Kong's capitalist economic system, its social system, and its "lifestyle" will be preserved for fifty years after 1997 under the formula of "one country, two systems." Finally, although the PRC will select Hong Kong's future government leaders, "Hong Kong people will govern Hong Kong."

The way in which the joint declaration was negotiated and ratified undermined popular confidence in both the agreement and the Hong Kong government. The negotiations were conducted in secret between representatives of the British and Chinese governments; Chinese authorities successfully excluded both the Hong Kong government and the people of Hong Kong by arguing that since Hong Kong people are Chinese, the Chinese government represented them. The people of Hong Kong did not participate in the negotiations over their future.

Once concluded, the agreement was put to the people of Hong Kong for their comment. No referendum or official poll was conducted on the agreement, but the Hong Kong government set up a small assessment office to receive and evaluate written submissions from the public. The British authorities, however, announced that the population of Hong Kong must accept the agreement in toto and without amendment; otherwise the colony would go into 1997 without any agreement at all. Not surprisingly, the people of Hong Kong accepted the agreement as better than nothing. In this they were placed in an extraordinarily difficult position. On the one hand, as opinion polls in the early 1980's clearly demonstrated, the people of Hong Kong wanted a continuation of the status quo, including a capitalist economic system, minimal government, and freedoms of the press and association. On the other hand, as Chinese they could not deny the PRC's claims to sovereignty over Hong Kong, nor could they support British colonialism.

By granting the PRC sole responsibility for drafting a Basic Law to govern Hong Kong after 1997, the agreement effectively curtailed the Hong Kong government's authority to make political reforms or constitutional changes during the transition period. The 1984 agreement was, then, a major blow to the autonomy of the colonial state. It created a fully legitimate shadow government, symbolized by the presence of the PRC's official representative in Hong Kong, the New China News Agency. The Hong Kong government, colonial officials' protests to the contrary, became a lame duck.

The reactions of strategic groups in Hong Kong varied. Many of the previously co-opted business elite, including T. S. Lo, T. K. Ann, and Sir Y. K. Pao, allied themselves with the Chinese government. They had benefited from the PRC's "open door" policies and economic modernization program, feared that middle-class proposals to expand political participation in Hong Kong would mean more social welfare and higher taxes, and hoped to rule the territory after 1997. Chinese authorities co-opted many of these business leaders onto its Basic Law Drafting Committee.

The middle class, especially the rapidly expanding professional cohort, reacted differently. Some demanded more participation in state decision-making in the run-up to 1997. Others protested that the PRC's new Basic Law for Hong Kong, passed by the Chinese National People's Congress in April 1990, seemed to undermine the territory's autonomy. In large numbers they elected to emigrate.

This response was, in part, the result of the government's own actions. In early 1984, to prepare public opinion in Hong Kong for the agreement that would follow, British authorities promised a more representative government for Hong Kong. This promise raised expectations, especially among liberal, middle-class pressure groups.

In their view the need to democratize became all the more urgent after the Sino-British agreement sealed Hong Kong's fate. The authorities held the first-ever elections of members to the Legislative Council in 1985, but the elections were organized by functional constituencies (the medical and legal professions, commerce and industry, teachers, and similar groups), and indirectly through district boards, in such a way that 99% of the population of Hong Kong were excluded from voting.

Promises from the government for a review of the system in 1987 fueled a middle-class campaign for more direct elections in 1988. The PRC protested that such elections would fundamentally alter the political status quo in Hong Kong, however, and local business elites sided with Chinese authorities to restrict the franchise. The British and Hong Kong authorities backed down.

Some middle-class groups have subsequently gone outside the restrictive, formally established political channels to express their commitment to democracy. On two occasions in May 1989 more than one million people marched through the streets of Hong Kong to show solidarity with democracy advocates in Beijing and to oppose the imposition of martial law there. The message to Hong Kong policy makers was clear—there was broad support for more representative government.

Middle-class professionals were also critical of features of the Basic Law governing post-1997 Hong Kong. They argued that it undermined Hong Kong's "high degree of autonomy" and gave too much power to the central government in Beijing by entrusting final interpretation of the Basic Law to the Standing Committee of the National People's Congress (that is, to the Chinese Communist Party Politburo or, in significant cases, its patrons—Chen Yun, Deng Xiaoping, Peng Zhen, and other "retired" elders) rather than to a local independent supreme court. Critics argued, too, that the legislature to be set up under the Basic Law would be too weak to achieve either democracy or locally accountable government. The Beijing-appointed Basic Law Drafting Committee brushed these criticisms aside.

Uneasy about their future under Chinese rule, some members of Hong Kong's middle class have emigrated to Canada, Australia, and the United States. Many, having left the PRC to come to Hong Kong, had been emigrants before. Since 1980 the number of Hong Kong residents leaving the territory for permanent resettlement overseas has skyrocketed. In 1990 alone authorities estimate that 62,000 will have left the territory; in the eight years leading up to 1997, about a half a million people are likely to have moved overseas. The "brain drain" has hit organizations employing skilled middle-class professionals the hardest. Hong Kong's economic success depends heavily on this strategic group.

Until the 1980's the colonial state was able to preserve relative political stability by co-opting strategic groups and redistributing benefits to the disadvantaged. The unwillingness or inability of the government now to accommodate the demands of the new middle class for more democracy is potentially destabilizing, and is likely to have long-term negative implications for Hong Kong's economic growth.

Conclusion: 1997 and Beyond

As with the other minidragons, Hong Kong's future economic growth depends on the interaction of external and internal factors; in this case, however, the 1997 issue has blurred the boundary between the external and the internal. Clearly external are developments among Hong Kong's competitors and in overseas markets. Competition from the other minidragons and political uncertainties in Hong Kong have encouraged Hong Kong's entrepreneurs to look for investment opportunities overseas, especially to Thailand, Malaysia, and Indonesia, but also to the Philippines, where land and labor costs are lower. Manufacturers have already benefited significantly from moving some operations to the PRC. In addition, protectionist pressures in the United States and other major markets like the EEC are likely to continue and perhaps even intensify during economic recessions. Competitive and protectionist pressures will probably cause manufacturing in Hong Kong to continue to decline. At the same time the territory's structural shift to financial services is likely to continue, though Japan's strong economy and its development into a major financial center will probably relegate Hong Kong to a subregional role.

An additional external factor, at least for the next few years, is Hong Kong's relationship with the PRC. Hong Kong is heavily dependent on the PRC for basic necessities such as food and water. But the PRC is increasingly exerting economic and political influence in other ways as well through heavy investment in Hong Kong real estate, banks, and trading and manufacturing companies. Economists estimate that by the late 1980's, Chinese investments in Hong Kong had totalled between US\$ 4 to US\$ 6 billion, of which more than US\$ 300 million was invested in manufacturing. Many of these investments have been in key sectors of the economy. Chinese International Trust and Investment Corporation (CITIC), for example, now has major shareholdings in Cathay Pacific Airways, Dragonair, Hong Kong Telephone, Tylfull, the Asiasat satellite consortium, and the Eastern Cross Harbor Tunnel. Along with CITIC, the Bank of China Group, the China Resources Group, the China Merchants Group, Everbright Corporation, and many other Chinese central and provincial enterprises have spread the web of the PRC's state capitalism into Hong Kong.

The PRC's state-capitalist actors are being co-opted into the local system of public policy making in Hong Kong. In many public policy arenas where implementation depends on the cooperation of a strategic group, the Hong Kong government has established a joint public-private consultative committee; the Aviation Advisory Board, the Port Committee, the Marketing Advisory Board, and the Transport Advisory Committee are examples. As the PRC's state-capitalist organizations control a larger part of the economy in the territory, they can be expected to join these committees; state policy in Hong Kong will increasingly be made in cooperation with the bureaucracies of the PRC.

The PRC's state capitalism in Hong Kong takes direction from mainland-based party-state bureaucracies, and there is consequently a very real potential for it to behave differently from private capitalism in the hands of private entrepreneurs. As long as the PRC directs its agencies to maximize profits and otherwise play by the rules of the game in Hong Kong, its participation will serve economic growth. Market distortions could result, however, if the PRC directs its agencies to disregard profit considerations and instead serve political goals such as the reunification of the PRC and Taiwan or the reward or punishment of political friends and enemies. There is already some evidence of this kind of behavior. For example, Chinese investment in failing but politically significant enterprises in Hong Kong such as the Conic Group of companies, electronic component producers that have had close ties to Taiwan, can be seen in this light.

The PRC's policies for the future of Hong Kong will also play a role in the territory's continued economic development. We can look for clues in the Basic Law, which will govern Hong Kong after 1997. To a large degree the Basic Law protects those features of the Hong Kong system that have previously spurred economic growth. The document upholds Hong Kong's capitalist economic system (Article 5); protects private property (Article 6); and endorses "minimalist" government, low taxes, free trade, balanced budgets, and lack of exchange controls (Articles 107, 109, 110, 112, and 114). Hong Kong's entrepreneurs are free from special restrictions, Hong Kong's laborers at liberty to pursue material wealth.

These policies are at sharp variance with the practice on the mainland, where party-state intervention in the economy is pervasive, the legal system is very weak, and bureaucrats control, suppress, and feed off entrepreneurs. Powerful conservative party leaders in the PRC denounce "bourgeois liberalism" and the unbridled pursuit of profit. Hong Kong's ability to maintain its political autonomy from the Chinese authorities will be critical; unfortunately, in their emphasis on regaining and exercising sovereignty over Hong Kong, the provisions of the Basic Law do not sufficiently provide for the "high degree of autonomy" promised in the Sino-British Joint Declaration. In particular the Basic Law gives the Chinese Communist Party (CCP) control over the selection of Hong Kong's legislature and most senior state officials, so although Hong Kong's first chief executive and legislature will be chosen by a selection committee comprising representatives of various strategic groups in Hong Kong, the committee will be chosen indirectly by the CCP. Complicated arrangements for the selection of subsequent chief executives and legislatures are designed to frustrate, not extend, democratic elections. Instead they will leave the CCP in Hong Kong in a powerful position of control.

Apart from undermining autonomy, these arrangements are destabilizing in two respects. They do not accommodate demands of Hong Kong's middle class for a more representative government, but appear rather to place control in the hands of functional constituencies, while in reality leaving the local CCP in a very strong position. Further, the arrangements integrate Hong Kong into mainland-based inner-party politics, a fact that could have destabilizing consequences. Because political institutions are very weak and the rule of law is underdeveloped in the PRC, factional struggles for political power are the norm. These can have violent outcomes, as the world saw in the events in Beijing on June 3–4, 1989. The PRC's unstable political regime will be imported into Hong Kong through the arrangements of the Basic Law.

Political stability may turn out to be the most critical factor in Hong Kong's economic future. As we have seen, the colonial government's ability to maintain relative political stability has been a key ingredient in Hong Kong's economic success so far. Recent surveys indicate that foreign investors in Hong Kong rate political stability as the most important factor in evaluating Hong Kong's investment environment, and that nearly 40% of respondents now rate that factor as unfavorable. Many influential people in Hong Kong would undoubtedly concur. Political stability in the territory can be maintained only by increasing the scope of political participation in response to popular demands. Thus Hong Kong's continued economic growth will depend as much on political reform as on economic factors. A relatively autonomous Hong Kong within the PRC is a prerequisite for these reforms.

Hong Kong's ability to maintain such limited autonomy after 1997 will depend on two major factors. If the Chinese leadership is relatively unified and aggressive in pursuing a policy of economic development rather than concentrating its energy on succession struggles, the stamping out of "bourgeois liberalism," or demonstrations of nationalism, then Hong Kong might be able to preserve its limited autonomy by making a significant contribution to the PRC's economic development program. Indeed, the territory has already done so: from 1979 to 1984 Hong Kong supplied about 20% of the PRC's net foreign exchange. If Hong Kong can continue to meet a significant portion of the PRC's foreign exchange needs, policy makers in Beijing will have an incentive to maintain the "two systems."

The other factor is Taiwan. Reunification of the PRC and Taiwan has continued to elude the Beijing government. In recent years, it has offered Taiwan a future which in many respects is like that promised to Hong Kong. If the PRC can recover sovereignty over Hong Kong without either economic setbacks for the territory or widespread political instability, its chances of reaching some kind of accommodation with Taiwan will be improved. In other words, the wish to demonstrate its sincerity towards Taiwan might provide a second incentive for China's leadership to grant greater autonomy to Hong Kong.

Hong Kong's autonomy, then, depends more on the perceptions of the leaders in Beijing than on the strength of the PRC's political institutions or on the Basic Law. Hong Kong's political position in the PRC will be relatively weak. As has been the case so often throughout its short history, Hong Kong will have to rely on the strength and adaptability of its vibrant economy to see it through troubled times.

South Korea:
The Challenge of Democracy

Chong-Sik Lee

*O*nly four decades ago General Charles G. Helmick told his colleagues in Washington that South Korea could never attain a high standard of living. Helmick knew the country well—he had served in Seoul as deputy military governor of the American occupation forces in South Korea after 1945—and the reasons for his prognosis were obvious. "There are virtually no Koreans with the technical training and experience required to take advantage of Korea's resources and effect an improvement over its present rice economy status," he said. He could have added that the artificial division of Korea by the United States and the Soviet Union after the country's liberation from Japan made it impossible for South Korea to survive as an independent economic entity. Helmick predicted that when the American occupation forces withdrew and stopped supplying South Korea, the country would be reduced to a "bull-cart" economy, and that some nine million non-food producers would face starvation. South Korea became independent in August 1948. The United States withdrew its troops in 1949.

In the summer of 1950 the Korean War broke out, and the situation became even bleaker. Civilian and military casualties mounted on both sides as cities and villages were turned into battle fronts, destroying much of the nation's infrastructure. The South Koreans who survived had little hope for a decent standard of living. The nation remained divided, the two hostile regimes confronting each other with large armies; and North Korea controlled all of the nation's mineral resources and the vestiges of the heavy industry that the Japanese colonialists had built.

Helmick's predictions were, of course, confounded. South Korea's is no longer a rice economy; the days are long gone when South Koreans flattened castoff oil drums to build buses that ran on rebuilt truck engines discarded by the military.

Chong-Sik Lee teaches in the political science department at the University of Pennsylvania. He is the author of numerous books and articles on Korea as well as on Asian politics and international relations. His most recent publications include *Korea Briefing 1990, In Search of a New Order in East Asia* and *North Korea in Transition*.

Notes for this chapter can be found on pages 191–192.

Today South Korea operates one of the world's most efficient steel industries, its shipyards build the world's largest oil tankers and ships, and it is a leading international exporter of automobiles, computers, and electronic equipment. In 1945 the country had only one university and a few colleges. Today the more than one hundred universities in South Korea contribute to one of the finest educational systems in the late-developing countries. In 1960 South Korea's per capita GNP was about $675. By 1989 it had reached $4,550. Finally, in just over two decades the average life expectancy of South Koreans has risen from fifty-eight to seventy years.

Much has been written about the reasons for South Korea's economic success. Some cited Korea's Confucian background as an advantage. Its stress on education facilitated the growth of the technically trained personnel to plan and implement economic growth. The authoritarian tradition allowed the emergence of an interventionist state that adopted a strongly outward-oriented foreign trade strategy and also permitted a strong-willed and determined leader to turn the bureaucracy into an instrument of economic growth.

Others have cited South Korea's favorable international environment. The world economy was on the rise just as the nation launched its export expansion. South Korea's principal ally, the United States, assisted its postwar economic recovery and offered a market to absorb South Korean exports. South Korea could also draw upon the experience and technology of Japan, the neighbor that had once dominated Korea as its imperial master. Some have even cited the Korean War as a stimulant to South Korea's growth as it provided an "international shock" to propel the people out of complacency and stimulated a strong sense of competition with the Communist North.

Geography and History

Many of the factors that contributed to the rapid postwar growth of South Korea's economy, then, were common to a number of countries in the region. But the operation of these factors in South Korea's unique natural and historical environment shaped the development of South Korea in a particular way. It would be a distortion, therefore, to cite the causes of the country's economic success in the abstract without paying sufficient attention to the environmental factors.

One of the natural conditions enabling the South Korean government to intervene economically with such success is that Korea is a small country. Located on a peninsula protruding southward from the northeastern corner of the Asian continent, this small country was artificially divided into two halves in 1945. As of

1990 South Korea's population numbered approximately 42 million people living in an area roughly the size of the state of Indiana.

Until 1945 Korea had had a long history as an integrated nation. The Korean people trace their origins to the founding of the state of Choson by the mythical god-man Tan'gun in 2,333 B.C. on the banks of the Taedong River in the northwest portion of the peninsula. While many historians are dubious about the historical accuracy of this account, there is a consensus that the kingdom of Choson was founded many centuries before Christ by the Yemaek tribe, which was related to other tribes living in northern and northeastern China. The Koreans thus have a long history as an independent people sharing a common history, a common language, and a common culture, a shared inheritance which has fostered a strong sense of national identity.

The Koreans survived as a nation against overwhelming odds. Their national identity was nearly obliterated in the thirteenth century by Mongol invaders, and again in the twentieth by a Japanese colonial government determined to blot out every trace of the Korean nation, including its language. But the Koreans survived. There is no doubt that nationalism is a source of South Korea's underlying strength.

Korea has also had a long history as a Confucian nation. Choson, the dynasty that existed in Korea from 1392 until it was conquered by Japan in 1910, was a quintessentially Confucian dynasty. Previous dynasties had espoused Buddhism, a dominant influence on the peninsula from its introduction in A.D. 372, but the new Confucian rulers determinedly purged Buddhism as heresy. The teachings of Confucius as interpreted by Zhu Xi became the officially sponsored dogma. Confucianism naturally left many legacies, both negative and positive.

One of the negative Confucian legacies has been intolerance of opposing views. The official-scholars of the Choson dynasty often engaged one another in bitter disputes about the correct interpretation of the masters, impugning opponents as heretics with evil intentions. The Koreans have been slow to develop the art of compromise. This has been the case not only in South Korea, but in the communist North as well; an astute observer has aptly referred to North Korea as a country under "Confucian Communism."

On the positive side, the Koreans have come to lay strong emphasis on learning. Passing civil service examinations based on Confucian teachings was traditionally the only avenue for social and economic advancement, and even today the Koreans attach supreme value to formal education. Education, indeed, is essential if one is to advance in the society, and the intense desire for advancement is shared by Koreans of all walks of life.

Confucianism attached enormous value to the power and status that accompanied government positions. Those with power enjoyed land ownership, the only form of wealth available to people living under a dynastic system that did not allow the emergence of a rich merchant class. The desire for status and social recognition remains strong among South Koreans; the intensity of competition observers remark on in the country today can be attributed to their never-ending search for higher social status.

The Confucian stress on human bonds and on duties and obligations has left both positive and negative legacies. Individual units (such as factories) and society as a whole can readily maintain cohesion and order because of the Koreans' ingrained sense of deference and mutual obligation, an element of the Confucian legacy that rulers and employers have often exploited for their own ends. But the emphasis on family bonds and obligations has also promoted nepotism, cronyism, and selfishness among individuals who are family oriented.

Confucianism has also left a legacy of the primacy of the centralized state and its bureaucracy. The Confucian teachings justified, indeed mandated, that the king should concern himself with all aspects of the lives of his subjects. The king's agents—government officials—were held superior in position, status, and, because they had passed the civil service examinations, intellect. The high prestige enjoyed by government officials made it easier to recruit the best educated and best trained Koreans for government service. This legacy might be said to have served the cause of an interventionist state, but it left few avenues by which society could check abuses of power, particularly when the government was headed by dictators.

The kingdom of Choson fell victim to Japanese imperialism in 1910, and Japan ruled Korea as a colonial power until 1945. Japanese colonialism left its own legacy in Korea.

While Japanese and Korean scholars assess the Japanese colonial era very differently, a few facts stand out. There is no doubt, for example, that the Koreans suffered much under the Japanese rule. During the Japanese occupation land ownership among the Koreans substantially decreased. The number of Koreans classified as poor increased from 11.2% of the total population in 1926 to 25.5% in 1937. The proportion of tenant farmers or sharecroppers rose from 35.2% in 1914 to 53.8% in 1942, and by 1945 per capita consumption of food grains had fallen from its 1910 level by nearly half. After 1937, when the Japanese launched their expansionist drive toward China and the Pacific, their rule in Korea was particularly harsh. But it is true also that the Japanese built in their colony a modern industrial infrastructure, albeit one intended to serve the needs of the empire. Most of the factories and other facilities were destroyed during the Korean War, but the foundation for modern industries remained. More important for later South Korean development, however, was the intimate knowledge acquired by Korean elites of the Japanese pattern of political and economic development. It was no accident that

President Park Chung Hee closely patterned his developmental strategy after that of Meiji Japan (1868–1912), and that the reasons for South Korea's success that we have discussed so far could be equally applied to an analysis of Japanese development during the Meiji era.

Japanese rule reinforced some of the legacies handed down from the Korean dynasties. The state, for instance, continued its primacy. The colonial government simply reinforced and modernized it. The state also came to play a more active role in running Korea's economy, allocating the colony's resources to suit the requirements of the Japanese empire. The colonial government, in fact, took total control of Korea's resources and labor during Japan's involvement in the Second World War, establishing a regime nominally headed by Emperor Hirohito and administered by the National Federation for the General Mobilization of the Subjects (Kokumin Sodoin Renmei). More than two decades later President Park, who borrowed heavily from Japanese policies, launched a similar movement in South Korea.

The colonial government also reinforced Confucian tradition in Korea. After the Meiji Restoration in Japan in 1868, the new state adopted Confucianism as the basic instrument of mobilizing popular support. In later years the Japanese were to pursue a similar policy in their Korean colony. The colonial period also intensified the Koreans' respect and desire for education. The Japanese took over Korea just as young Koreans had begun to realize their need for modern education and had organized a nationwide campaign urging the establishment of schools teaching Western curricula. The demise of the Korean kingdom only spurred them on.

Opportunities for modern education, however, were severely limited. The colonial government did increase the number of primary and secondary schools, but at a very slow rate. By 1944, the year before the Japanese left Korea, only 7.1% of the Korean population had graduated from elementary school, and fewer than 1% had finished middle school.

Japan's defeat by the Allies in World War II brought an end to Japanese colonial rule, but it also led to the artificial division of Korea at the 38th parallel. The United States proposed the division after the Soviet Union declared war against Japan on August 8, 1945, and began military operations in Korea. Having watched the Soviets install puppet governments in Eastern Europe, American leaders were anxious to prevent the Soviet Union from occupying the entire peninsula. Growing Cold-War conflict between the two superpowers led to the establishment in 1948 of two regimes with separate capitals in Seoul and Pyongyang. The northern regime is known as the Democratic People's Republic of Korea, the southern regime as the Republic of Korea (ROK).

The division of the country proved to be the prelude to the Korean War (1950–53), which brought nothing but misery and destruction. Although the fighting ended in a truce in 1953, two large, modern armies still confront each other along a truce line established near the original line of division at the 38th parallel. The division placed South Korea in an unenviable position economically. North Korea possessed most of the peninsula's mineral resources, as well as "75 per cent of the total industrial output of Korea." South Korea was left with its rice farms and with light industries that had depended on the North for heavy industrial products and electricity. At the time of partition, the fact that South Korea had approximately twice the population of the North was certainly not an advantage.

The war, of course, meant senseless destruction of lives and property, but it did serve to expedite the process of national integration within South Korea. The movement of a vast number of refugees over a three-year period broke down many of the regional and urban-rural barriers. Rural youths who might have endured lives as underprivileged farmers of narrow experience and views were suddenly forced to broaden their perspectives as they mingled with their urban counterparts in running modern equipment and organizations. The war was a tremendous equalizer: virtually everyone was reduced to the status of paupers. South Koreans could not have survived without the continuous and substantial financial aid provided by the United States and other members of the United Nations.

United States' troops landed in Korea after the Japanese surrender in 1945. American leaders decided in mid-1947 that the peninsula was of no vital strategic importance to the United States, however, and that the cost of defending it against Soviet attack would be disproportionate to its value. This analysis derived from the facts that the Korean peninsula was a part of the Asian continent and that the entire continent was about to yield to communist control. Both military and congressional leaders in the United States publicly announced that Korea was outside of the American defense perimeter in the Pacific, and that there was little likelihood that the United States would confront communist forces even if Korea were attacked. Even though the establishment of the ROK in 1948 had the blessing of the Americans, the United States nevertheless pulled its troops out of Korea in 1949.

The North Korean attack against South Korea in June 1950 provoked an abrupt reversal in American policy on Korea, however, and the United States deployed a massive military force to engage the North Korean and Chinese forces. President Truman viewed the attack as part of a Soviet design to encroach on United States-supported regimes throughout the world. According to this analysis the United States could ill afford to ignore so stark a challenge without damaging its prestige, for even though the United States had not concluded a defense treaty with the ROK, there was no question that the South Korean government had been created with its blessing.

In the course of the Korean War, the relationship between South Korea and the United States broadened. American economic advisers came to play a crucial role in South Korea's economic planning, and the Americans provided substantial aid to finance postwar reconstruction. They also sent military aid—twice as much in value as their economic aid. Finally, even after the truce was signed in 1954, American troops remained stationed in South Korea; as of 1990 they numbered approximately 40,000.

Even though the battles ended in 1954 with the signing of the truce agreement at Panmunjom, the confrontation with the North continued. The truce line has been impregnable; for over three decades not a single piece of private mail crossed the line. North-South talks begun in 1972 have failed to dissipate tensions. In September 1985 fifty lucky individuals each from North and South Korea were allowed to hold family reunions under the auspices of the two governments (the experiment has not been repeated). In late 1990 the premiers of the two regimes exchanged visits to find a way to reduce tension, but the relationship between the two regimes remains volatile.

North Korea insists that tensions can be reduced only if American forces are withdrawn and armies on both sides are substantially reduced. The South Korean leaders have interpreted this demand as a scheme to weaken South Korea's defenses, and have called instead for trade, exchanges of visits, and other North-South contacts to build an atmosphere of trust so that military questions can be discussed in earnest.

Mutual fears and suspicions have prevented the two sides from engaging in meaningful discourse. South Korea has been concerned about North Korea's repeated call for socialist and communist revolution throughout the peninsula, a call broadcast and published in the North Korean media as late as 1990. Commando and terrorist attacks launched as recently as 1987 against the South Korean presidential palace, presidential retinue abroad (in Rangoon, Burma), and passenger airplanes have not improved North Korea's image. For their part, the North Koreans fear that American and South Korean forces may launch a surprise attack against the North.

The confrontation with North Korea has deeply affected South Korea's political and economic development. In the face of the threat from the Communist dictatorship to the North, the South Korean government has regarded security as its primary concern, leading to the suppression of all elements even remotely associated with communism. Intellectuals, journalists, and politicians have always had to walk a narrow line between permissible and impermissible behavior. The government has strictly controlled labor unions; the Communist Party completely dominated the labor movement before the ROK was established in 1948, and the new government in the south was unwilling to let the enemy infiltrate the movement again.

The enormous power of the South Korean government has attracted to politics and public service a large number of strong-willed men who have contested for power whenever opportunities arose. The authoritarian tradition of Korea and the predilections of politicians to maximize their gains, however, have largely confined South Korea to authoritarian regimes.

It is ironic that Syngman Rhee, the first president of the republic, is now known as a dictator. In his youth he was an ardent advocate of democratic reforms; he was imprisoned for his radicalism between 1899 and 1904. He spent much of his life in exile in Hawaii, where he experienced democracy at first hand. But in order to assure his reelection, he declared martial law in 1952 and forced the unwilling members of the national assembly to approve an amendment to the constitution. The constitution was amended again in 1955 by the use of strong-arm tactics to allow Rhee to succeed himself indefinitely.

During its early years the ROK made somewhat fitful economic progress. Most South Koreans were pessimistic about the possibility of economic development in their country. South Korea was poor in natural resources, and American aid was insufficient to fully offset the economic burden of maintaining a large army. President Rhee's primary concern was the reunification of Korea: for him, focussing on the economic development of South Korea would have been tantamount to admitting defeat in the unification effort. Rhee insisted that the United States provide him with arms to continue the war to reunify the country, and refused to send official representatives to the truce talks at Panmunjom in 1953.

The Rhee regime did face the enormous task of reconstructing the war-torn economy, however, and the years between 1953 and 1958 were devoted to reconstruction with aid provided by the United States and the UN reconstruction agency. The government pursued a policy of import-substituting industrialization (ISI), attempting to increase industrial production by emphasizing light industrial products for domestic consumption. Light manufactures, including textiles, food, beverages, tobacco, wood, leather, and paper, dominated the early stages of South Korean industrialization. GNP rose by an average of 5.5% a year from 1954 through 1958, industrial production leading the advance with an annual growth rate of nearly 14%.

By 1958, however, the economy had lost its momentum. The saturation of the domestic market, growing unemployment, and difficulties in obtaining foreign exchange for necessary imports led the government to review the wisdom of its import-substituting development strategy. The government was also concerned with arresting inflation and coping with sharply reduced aid from the United States.

However, political factors were also responsible for the slowdown. Rhee was aging; his chosen right-hand man was in ill health. By 1958 Rhee's underlings were paying more attention to political survival than to economic development. In 1960, for the first time in South Korean history, the government adopted a comprehensive seven-year economic development plan, but the plan was not a high priority for the aging and increasingly corrupt Rhee regime.

Authoritarianism and Economic Development: The Regime of Park Chung Hee, 1961–79

Rhee's regime was overthrown by a student revolt in 1960, and South Korea experienced a democratic interlude that proved to be short lived. The following year a military junta under Major General Park Chung Hee overthrew the democratic regime and instituted a junta government. In 1963 Park was elected president under a new constitution; he ruled as president until he was assassinated in 1979. Like Rhee, Park had the constitution amended in 1972 to succeed himself indefinitely. Both men considered themselves indispensable to national security and prosperity.

It was the Park regime (1961–79) that presided over South Korea's phenomenal economic growth. South Korea's growth rate during these years was virtually unmatched anywhere else and has been the subject of numerous studies. If Syngman Rhee had been an ideologue who dedicated most of his life to fighting Japan and communism, Park and his officials were pragmatists. Park rejected the idea of unifying the country through war; he called instead for an incremental improvement of relations with North Korea. Rhee had insisted that Japan apologize and compensate South Korea for the atrocities committed during its thirty-six-year rule of Korea, and was generally negative toward resuming relations; the Park regime was more willing to compromise. Rhee saw nothing in Japan's past and present but evil; Park saw a model for South Korean development. Park also wanted to free South Korea from its overwhelming dependence on the United States for aid and trade and to improve ties with Japan, Europe, and the Third World.

Park and the young military men who took power in 1961 were similar to Rhee, however, in their political and administrative inexperience. And they lacked a development program of their own. The junta also found the task of managing a national economy daunting. Park's government therefore focused on economic goals, and it turned to professionals to help achieve them. Park deserves credit for providing firm political support for the work of the professionals and for making some crucial developmental decisions.

Park's most important institutional innovation was his creation of the Economic Planning Board (EPB) in May 1964. The EPB was directed by the deputy prime minister, who was given broad fiscal, financial, and economic powers. It controlled both budget and planning functions as well as the allocation of foreign aid. The EPB became the central source and clearing house for all economic policy. Its powers were later broadened to encompass the monetary and fiscal measures, institutional changes, and policies that were needed not only to make stabilization efforts more effective, but also to support a more aggressive growth policy. Park's new development policy was based on an overall strategy of export oriented industrialization (EOI), although it retained some of the protectionist components of ISI.

Some of the measures undertaken by the EPB in the period that followed were revolutionary in the Korean context. In May 1964 the EPB devalued the currency, the *won,* by 90% and established a unitary exchange rate. The *won* was floated in 1965. Exports had more than doubled between 1961 and 1963, and they rose another 50% in 1964; government emphasis on exports began to play a dominant role in economic, including investment, policy. In 1965 the EPB drafted a more aggressive Second Five-Year Plan and began to liberalize import restrictions; the government put through an interest rate reform that revitalized the banking sector by attracting private savings with high interest rates.

In line with the strategy of EOI, the government also provided businesses with powerful incentives to export: they were given preferential treatment in obtaining low-interest bank loans, import privileges which included permission to borrow from foreign sources, and tax benefits. These incentives were particularly important because of the large differential between bank loans and private loans. Because of their scarcity, imported products commanded high prices in the domestic market. Import privileges were doubly profitable because they were accompanied by government-guaranteed foreign loans which bore very low interest rates relative to domestic rates. Would-be entrepreneurs needed virtually no capital to start businesses, and the opportunities were enormous. South Koreans responded eagerly to the incentives, meeting the government's export targets.

Park's strategy was thus to guide, encourage, and support private entrepreneurs. If his politics could be characterized as "guided democracy," his economics were "guided economic development." Under strong and direct encouragement from the state, some of South Korea's most successful businesses grew into *chaebol,* or huge conglomerates. The *chaebol* emerged as the distinctive hallmark of South Korean industrialization, dominating the nation's economy. Further, in the years to come conglomerates such as Hyundai, Samsung, Daewoo, and Kumsong (gold star) would be the most recognizable symbols of South Korea's place in the world economy.

The two Chinese characters that form the word *chaebol* in the Korean language form *zaibatsu* in Japanese. These organizations not only share the same Chinese word, but their historical origins are similar. Both South Korean and Japanese conglomerates began with small nuclear enterprises that benefited from government contacts and patronage. Both were given government protection that enabled them to monopolize certain spheres of activity and thereby accumulate capital to finance diversification into other areas. One crucial difference between *chaebol* and *zaibatsu*, however, is that the Japanese conglomerates have their own banks and finance their operations internally, while the *chaebol* have had to depend on government-guaranteed external financing—the South Korean government has prevented them from acquiring banks for fear of their disrupting the free flow of capital. The *chaebol* are therefore more vulnerable than their Japanese counterparts to governmental pressures and the vicissitudes of international markets.

Park's developmental programs required enormous amounts of capital. Since the United States was no longer willing or able to sustain its previous level of assistance, the Park regime resorted to "financial diplomacy" elsewhere. The normalization of relations with Japan brought Japanese funds in the form of loans and compensation for the damage South Korea suffered during the colonial era. In late 1964 Park paid a state visit to the Federal Republic of Germany which led to government aid and commercial credits. The availability of foreign funds and its own increasing exports boosted South Korea's credit rating, enabling the country to borrow more on the open international market. Foreign loans played the key role in the initial stage of economic development. The success of South Korea's export drive derived from other factors as well, namely the availability of an educated labor force and the favorable international market. South Korea had made stunning advances in education since the liberation in 1945. From 1945 to 1965 enrollment in elementary schools rose from 1.3 million pupils to 3.6 million, in high schools from 50,000 to 164,000. Enrollments in vocational high schools increased fivefold, in institutions of higher learning by a factor of eighteen. The explosive rise in education reflected the success of government policy in encouraging the aspirations of the South Koreans.

Park's export drive fortuitously started when the world economy was booming. The world market was exploding between 1965 and 1975, the decade in which South Korea's exports expanded. The availability of the American and Japanese markets was of crucial importance to South Korean advancement. The United States absorbed a large share of South Korean products. In 1966 Japan surpassed the United States to become South Korea's largest trading partner, a position it has occupied ever since. The United States remained the largest purchaser of South Korean products until 1973, when Japan overtook the Americans by this measure as well, spending $1,242 million on South Korean goods (38.5% of total exports) to the United States' $1,021 million. Japan was also a major source of public and private loans to South Korea, providing $674 million in commercial loans and $416 million in government loans between 1965 and 1973.

Another factor helping South Korean exporters in the 1960's was that they faced little competition from other developing countries. South Korean industries were using entry-level technologies that were relatively easy to acquire and learn.

Many Japanese industries were preparing to install advanced technology, and they were eager to sell their old plants and technologies to South Korea.

The content of the rapidly growing exports was typical of the early stage of EOI. Manufactured goods constituted less than 20% of total exports before 1962, but increased to 41.5% in 1963 and 73.5% in 1968. Within this category light industrial products supplied the largest share of South Korea's exports. The emphasis was on items that would benefit from low wages and an unskilled labor force, in particular textiles, clothing, and footware. At the same time South Korean entrepreneurs were gaining more experience and preparing to diversify their commodities and markets.

As had always been the case in postwar Korea, however, the stimulus for economic change had to come from the state. In 1972 President Park launched the third five-year economic development plan (1972–1976), an ambitious program which sought to redress the imbalance caused by the first two five-year plans (1962–1971) by emphasizing the agricultural sector. The new plan also marked a reorientation of the nation's export strategy: it called for the development of heavy and chemical industries to better prepare South Korea for the intensified competition in the world market. In response to President Carter's announced plan to withdraw American ground troops from South Korea, the plan also looked to facilitate the domestic production of weaponry. In the early years of the 1970's, more than 50% of industrial investment in South Korea went into developing chemicals, petroleum products, and basic metals. The new policy had a direct impact on export structure. Electrical products and electronics, iron and steel, metalworks, and ships began to figure prominently in South Korea's exports. In 1980 heavy and chemical industries accounted for 44% of all export value and nearly half of all industrial exports. Four years earlier the ratio had been less than 30%. Under government prodding, efforts were thus made in the late 1970's to move South Korea away from its earlier dependence on labor intensive, low-value-added light industry.

The political consequences of Park's new emphasis on heavy and chemical industries were enormous. The allocation of exorbitant sums of capital to industries that required long gestation periods increased existing inflationary pressure. Small- and medium-sized manufacturers producing light industrial products suffered the most, and depressed output led to a shortage of consumer goods, a shortage exacerbated by increasing consumer demand brought about by rising wages and the advance in living standards. Price controls imposed on producers of consumer goods further discouraged the manufacturers. Meanwhile, the inflow of foreign loans to finance the new heavy and chemical industries rapidly expanded the money supply, further fueling inflation. According to a Bank of Korea report, consumer prices rose only 14.4% in 1978; most observers agreed that the actual rate was near 30%.

The high rate of inflation continued into 1979. The second oil shock that year aggravated Korea's problems. According to a report issued by the EPB in August 1979, the cost of living for the average household had gone up 26.3% since August 1978. Although wages had been rising very rapidly in previous years, spurred by shortages of skilled and semi-skilled workers, the rise in wages began to slow down. To cure these ills, in December 1978 the president replaced his economic team in the cabinet, including the vice premier in charge of economic planning, and adopted stabilization measures. The ensuing recession increased unemployment and produced a succession of bankruptcies among small- and medium-sized enterprises that were dependent on loans.

Park's emphasis on heavy and chemical industries reduced the power of the EPB to coordinate various sectors of the economy, because he had created a separate planning office, beyond the EPB's reach, for the Heavy and Chemical Industry Promotion Committee. The result was bitter bureaucratic conflicts. The EPB advocated tight monetary and fiscal policies, but these were incompatible with the government's new policy of promoting heavy and chemical industries.

In allowing the momentum of economic development to be lost in the late 1970's, President Park lost his strongest weapon against critics who abhorred his dictatorship. Park had revised the constitution in 1972 in order to consolidate power in his own hands. The 1972 constitution, known as the Yushin or Revitalization constitution, had granted the president authority and sole discretion to declare a state of emergency and had assigned him dictatorial powers. He was also authorized to nominate one-third of the members of the National Assembly; his candidates were to be "elected" by the hand-picked 2,359-member "National Conference for Unification." The president could succeed himself indefinitely by being "elected" by the same "Conference" without debate. Park used his new powers liberally. He issued decrees to silence all forms of opposition. Numerous dissidents were arrested and imprisoned, and the press was severely controlled. The KCIA extended its tentacles everywhere, even to South Koreans abroad, precipitating such international incidents as the kidnapping of Kim Dae-Jung from his Tokyo hotel. Kim had been Park's opponent in the presidential election of 1971 and had voiced his opposition to the 1972 constitution from abroad. Emergency Decree Number 9, issued on May 13, 1975, had made it a crime punishable by imprisonment of more than one year to criticize the constitution or report such criticisms.

The December 1978 general election for the National Assembly revealed Park's government to be a fragile system held in place by sheer force. This was the first general election since 1973, and in spite of all the handicaps of running an election in an authoritarian atmosphere, the opposition won a handsome plurality with 34.7% of the votes, an increase of 2.2% from 1973, while the government party's share declined to 30.9%. Independent candidates won 27.2% of votes, and most of them joined the opposition New Democratic Party. The majority of the voters clearly wanted a change.

The election results strengthened the cause of the opposition leader, Kim Young Sam, and in June 1979 he launched a scathing attack against the policies of the Park government. The government retaliated by removing Kim from the National Assembly, a measure that only intensified the highly charged political atmosphere. The workers and students soon joined in the struggle against the Park regime by taking to the streets, thus presenting the government with a dilemma. Applying more pressure on the opposition would create martyrs, making the situation even more explosive. Loosening control might foster the spread of demands for reform, rendering it impossible for the government to contain the opposition. Park's lieutenants were evidently divided on what measures would best manage the crisis. The director of the KCIA (Korean Central Intelligence Agency), Kim Jae-Kyu, shot President Park and the director of the presidential security forces dead on December 12, 1979, while they were deliberating these measures. Kim later told a military court that his victims wanted to resort to brutal force to suppress the demonstrators.

It can be argued that President Park drove himself onto the horns of a dilemma by instituting the Yushin system and wielding unlimited power. His political measures alienated a large number of South Koreans. The economic downturn brought political grievances into sharper focus and increased support for the opposition. The Yushin system may have been necessary to promote the heavy and chemical industries South Korea needed, but the system did not provide a safety valve for social and political pressures. It might have been maintained through manipulation of all the political and economic mechanisms, but government control of all these variables proved to be impossible.

The Transition to Democracy, 1979–90

Park's death and the subsequent removal of his key lieutenants from the scene ushered in a period of euphoria in which virtually everyone in South Korea anticipated the introduction of democracy. Former premier Choy Kyu Ha, who inherited President Park's position, reaffirmed the need for a new constitution in his inaugural speech in December 1979. He promised that a new constitution supported by a majority of the people would be adopted within a year, and that a fair general election would be held soon afterward. But Choy, a former bureaucrat without any political force behind him, lacked the means to deliver his promise.

A military junta headed by Major General Chun Doo Hwan made its power felt by arresting the incumbent chief of staff of the army in December 1979, finally taking over the government in May 1980. Chun was the head of the Defense Security

Agency, which oversaw internal security in the armed forces. Chun and his colleagues were not about to let the "corrupt politicians" rule the nation. Although a new constitution was adopted, the basic features of the political system that Park built remained in place, particularly the provision for the election of the president by the handpicked "National Conference for Unification." The only major difference was that the president was to be limited to a single seven-year term. The KCIA was discredited in the wake of its director's assassination of President Park, and the new military leaders relied on the Defense Security Agency to control the political arena and the society. The military thus continued to dominate politics.

Appealing to the slogan of creating a "just and wholesome society," the junta conducted a "clean-up campaign" with a vengeance. All political parties were dissolved. Most politicians were either prohibited from engaging in political activities or arrested. Some 170 periodical publications were summarily abolished, among them some of the finest liberal intellectual magazines. Private broadcasting stations were ordered to be merged. Professors and journalists of liberal leanings were removed from their positions. Numerous bureaucrats and bankers were fired. These acts of "cleansing" were accompanied by a massive re-education campaign aimed at the entire population. This New Community Training movement was headed by General Chun's younger brother Chun Kyong-hwan.

The new constitution adopted in September 1980 guaranteed basic freedoms and granted the National Assembly the power to enact laws, but the junta was not about to let parliamentarians direct the course of events. Before the constitution went into effect, the junta appointed a National Security Legislative Council, which enacted a plethora of laws with the proviso that they could not be amended by the National Assembly.

The Chun regime was never to win legitimacy from the public. It failed to win popular support in part because there was no plausible justification for the coup of May 1980. But Chun's Achilles' heel was the Kwangju Massacre of May 1980. The massacre occurred when "special forces," paratroopers dispatched by the Martial Law Command under Chun's control, brutally gunned down nearly two hundred citizens of Kwangju who had defied the military edict banning demonstrations. Chun's image suffered further in 1982 with the eruption of a financial scandal involving members of his family. A financier related to Chun's wife manipulated nearly US$ 1 billion, approximately 17% of South Korea's entire money supply, forcing some of the country's large corporations into bankruptcy. The incident also uncovered influence peddling and bribe taking by Mrs. Chun's uncle, who was alleged to have amassed hundreds of millions of dollars. Chun's pronouncements calling for a "just society" and the eradication of corruption simply could not be believed.

The public appeared to tolerate the prolonged military rule, however, particularly when President Chun repeatedly affirmed his desire to retire at the end of his term of office and set a precedent for a "peaceful transfer of power." But on his attempt in April 1987 to squash the opposition and install his hand-picked successor as president, the public reacted with universal outrage. Roh Tae Woo, whom Chun had chosen to succeed him, had been Chun's classmate at the Military Academy and a participant in the December 1978 coup. South Koreans were less concerned with his past than with the political mechanism proposed for his formal selection; they were incensed at the proposal that Roh be "elected" by the "National Reunification Council," a rubber-stamp body supporting those in power. Ordinary citizens, who had previously disdained the "radical" student opposition, joined in the anti-Chun demonstrations that erupted everywhere in the country.

On June 26, 1987, Roh Tae Woo made a dramatic announcement in which he supported a new democratic constitution that embodied all of the opposition's demands. The constitution was quickly amended, and there ensued a campaign for a popularly elected president, culminating in the election of December 16. Student agitation, popular discontent with military dictatorship, and the vulnerability of the Chun government all contributed to the fact that the election was held at all. But the opposition failed to win the election; their two principal candidates split the vote, and Roh won with a plurality of 36.6% of the votes cast. Kim Young Sam, the head of the New Democratic Party, won 28%, while Kim Dae-Jung came in third with 27%.

The failure of the opposition to present a consolidated front dealt a severe blow to the Kims, who had been at the forefront of movements against the South Korean dictatorship for two decades. They had repeatedly been urged to unite and had promised to do so, but they could not agree on the crucial question of who should become the presidential candidate of the united front. Neither candidate would withdraw from the candidacy, particularly because the prize they had fought for all their lives appeared to be so near at hand. The outcome was that the opposition lost the presidency with a combined vote of 55%; the Kims exchanged their lofty reputations as democratic heroes for less flattering ones, as the public came to see them simply as power-seeking politicians.

The Kims, however, were not to be dismissed out of hand. In the April 1988 elections for the National Assembly, the voters elected 71 candidates of Kim Dae-Jung's Party for Peace and Democracy and 59 candidates of Kim Young Sam's Reunification Democracy Party. Roh's Democratic Justice Party (DJP) won 125 seats, another party led by yet another Kim, former premier Kim Jong Pil, 35 seats. Despite its plurality, Roh's party was clearly short of a majority in the 299-seat parliament. Kim Jong Pil's New Democratic Republic Party was a logical ally of Roh's DJP, since

Kim Jong Pil had been a follower and a relative of the assassinated President Park. But there had been bad feelings between Kim Jong Pil and Roh, because the military leaders under Chun Doo Hwan had harshly treated Kim and his cohort. Roh therefore appeared to be destined to run the democratized nation with minority support.

These early years of the Roh regime turned out to be the most turbulent period in South Korean history. The new constitution, adopted by popular referendum, guaranteed people full freedoms, while the governing party lacked the majority vote in the National Assembly. More importantly, however, a paralysis of authority set in, not only in the political arena, but in the society as a whole.

South Korea had suffered traumatically during the 1970's under Park and Chun, more particularly under Chun. General Chun had offered high-minded ideals as the rationale for his military takeover in 1981, but had evolved into the most self-aggrandizing of rulers; the public lost its traditional esteem and respect for those who governed them. The failure of the two opposition leaders to unite against Roh in the 1987 election further disillusioned the South Koreans. The Roh government was very closely linked with the Chun regime, and hence bore some of the stigma attached to Chun. In spite of lengthy investigations, the government was unable to assign responsibility for the Kwangju incident to the public's satisfaction. Church leaders, the press, and the intellectuals had been co-opted by the Park and Chun regimes, and most of them were accustomed to serving the government's interest. The paralysis of authority that set in and intensified through the 1980's was a reaction against the long period of repression that had begun in 1972.

The high emotions of the period were reflected in the student and labor strikes that dominated the news between 1988 and 1989. Influenced by revisionist and Marxist historians, radical student leaders demanded rapid, if not radical, changes in the political and economic structure. Full of energy and curiosity, the students found evil everywhere, in politics, in foreign relations, in the economy, and in the social system. In their view South Korea clearly needed a revolution. Citing the American general's status as commander of the Joint U.S.-ROK military command, the students charged the American military command in South Korea with responsibility for the Kwangju incident. Some went even further, charging that the United States was an imperialist power occupying South Korea against the people's will. At the same time the workers were demanding their fair share of the expanded economy. They resorted to massive strikes, winning 50% to 60% wage increases in those two years. It was in this context that Roh and other politicians ran the "democratic experiment."

South Korea

South Korea's mountainous terrain is featured in many of its 17 national parks and 21 provincial parks.

Buddha's Birthday, the "Feast of the Lanterns," is celebrated by solemn rituals.

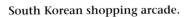

Seoul's business district at night.

South Korean shopping arcade.

Hyangwonjong Pavilion, part of the Kyongbokkung Palace complex, Seoul, first built in 1394 by King T'aejo, and rebuilt in the nineteenth century.

Mt. Soraksan (5,604 ft.) is located in Mt. Soraksan National Park, near the eastern port city of Sokch'o.

Women picking tomatoes.

A Korean fish market.

Cherry blossom time.

Patrols guarding the demilitarized zone separating North and South Korea.

Storage facilities for petrochemical products.

Tongdaemun (East Gate) Market silk shop.

A venerable gentleman in traditional clothing, including the "bird-cage hat" and white jacket made especially for patriarchs.

Students confront police in Seoul, June, 1989.

In the foreground is Namdaemun Gate, the South Gate, one of the five remaining of Seoul's original eight gates.

These *changsung*, or spirit posts, guard village entrances and passages leading to temples. They are considered intermediaries between earth and the beyond, and guardians of fortune.

Assembly of sub-miniature parts requires use of microscopes for magnification.

Automated integrated circuit production.

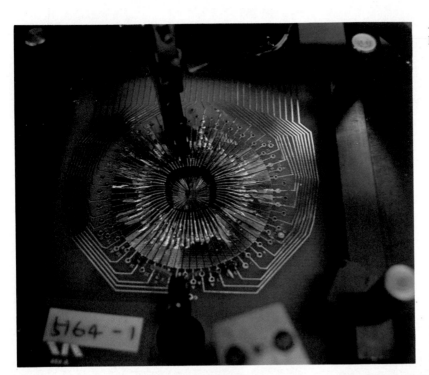

Factory workers at Ulsan Industrial Estate, a center of heavy industry.

Participants in new employee training program, SsangYong Business Group, South Korea.

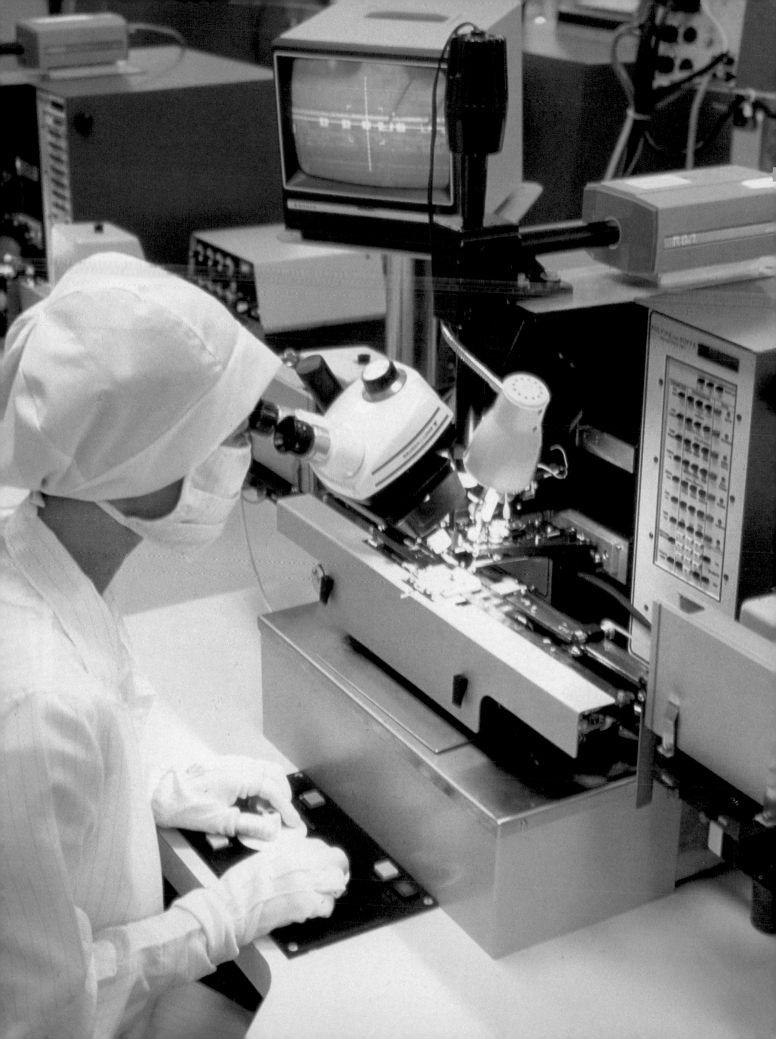

Robotics are used to perform welding operations on an automotive assembly line.

Wigs are processed at the Bando Trading Co. workshop.

A patchwork of cultivated farm land, South Korea.

Violence breaks out after South Korean elections.

Children look over the wreckage left by post-election violence.

The nation's first refrigerator-boat for deep-sea fishing, the 3,000-ton Kaeyang-ho.

The Daewoo conglomerate's shipbuilding facility at Okp'o on Koje Island near Pusan.

Buddhist statue in Sokkuram Grotto.

Detail of Korean architecture within the Kyongbokkung Palace compound, Seoul.

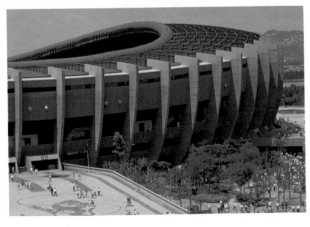

Part of the Olympic sports complex built by South Korea for the 1988 Games.

Roh made a dramatic gesture in January 1990 in announcing the formation of a new coalition party. Taking as their model Japan's Liberal Democratic Party, in which several factions compete within a single ruling party, Kim Young Sam's Reunification Democracy Party, Kim Jong Pil's new Democratic Republic Party, and the ruling DJP allied to form the new Democratic Liberal Party (DLP). The future of this coalition is by no means clear. An angry Kim Dae jung remains in opposition, and continued demonstrations as well as poor showings at supplementary elections held to fill vacant seats suggest that the popular appeal of the party is uncertain. Most important of all, clear divisions among the coalition partners suggest difficulties in reaching elite consensus and thus in formulating national policy. In this uncertain political environment, much of Roh Tae Woo's platform for change remains unrealized, and may remain so until the next elections for the national assembly and the presidency in 1992 and 1993.

In spite of these political problems, the regimes of Chun Doo Hwan and Roh Tae Woo can be credited with a few landmark achievements. One was the holding of the Olympic games in Seoul in 1988. Another was the success of their "Northern Policy" in establishing diplomatic relations with the Soviet Union and East European countries. While these events took place under the Roh regime, it was the Chun regime that had laid the groundwork.

The Chun regime deserves much credit for the Seoul Olympics, since it was Chun who won the right in 1981 to host the summer Olympics in 1988 and who undertook the task of preparing the nation for them. The preparation involved a major allocation of human and material resources. Sports arenas, lodging, and transportation facilities had to be built, rivers and harbors dredged and beautified, and above all, the South Korean people readied to welcome the onslaught of athletes and other visitors. The games were a phenomenal success. They provided South Korea with tangible long-term benefits in the form of infrastructure, but perhaps more important were the intangible benefits of improving the country's image internationally, boosting the self-confidence of the South Korean people, increasing foreign trade, and facilitating the success of the country's "Northern diplomacy."

Ironically, the Olympics contributed also to the military's decision to abdicate power and introduce democracy, and to the government's mellowing toward North Korea. As the date of the games approached, everyone in South Korea was aware that the country had become the center of the world's attention. The opposition took the opportunity offered by this international interest to become more vocal, particularly after Chun Doo Hwan's announcement in April 1987 that he had decided to "terminate the fruitless debate" concerning constitutional revision. Government officials who advocated harsh retaliation against the opposition were overruled; either continuing turmoil or severe repression would have jeopardized South

Korea's chance of holding the Olympics, a risk Chun was not prepared to take.

Similarly, for fear that North Korea might disrupt the Olympics, the government found it necessary to placate its northern neighbor. Roh's government attempted to induce the northern regime to participate in the Olympics either by joining with South Korea to form united Korean sports teams or by sending separate North Korean teams to the Olympics. President Roh also issued a declaration in July 1988, just two months prior to the opening of the Olympics, announcing his government's intention of regarding the northern regime as compatriots rather than mortal enemies; he declared his desire to assist rather than to hinder North Korea's effort to promote friendly ties with South Korea's allies. In December the Roh government reversed an important element of South Korea's military policy in declaring further its intention of discussing military matters with North Korea. While North Korea did not send any teams to the Olympics, there was no disruption of the games. And all these moves laid the ground both for the North-South Korean premiers' talks in September–October 1990 and for the Japanese rapprochement with North Korea that began in September 1990.

While there were other factors at play, the Olympics provided a major impetus for the Soviet Union and East European countries to improve their ties with South Korea. For the first time in their history, the Soviet Union and its allies sent large numbers of officials to South Korea to observe the country and to begin to establish unofficial trade and other relationships. These ties eventually led to the establishment of diplomatic relations between South Korea and these countries in 1989, and culminated in President Roh's meeting with President Gorbachev in San Francisco in May 1990. Over North Korea's protest, South Korea and the Soviet Union established a formal relationship in September 1990. Another achievement of the Chun Doo Hwan regime that Roh has sought to capitalize on was its success in restoring South Korea's confidence in economic growth. The quick economic turnaround brought about by the Chun regime clearly indicated that the South Korean economy had already established a firm foundation for growth in terms of its infrastructure, work force, and expertise.

In the late 1970's the Chun regime inherited an economy suffering from the side effects of Park's policy of building up chemical and heavy industries, and the new government therefore concentrated on stabilization. Credit was tightened. The bureaucratic disorientation created by the establishment of the independent Planning Office of Heavy and Chemical Industries Promotion Committee was remedied by restoring the power of the Economic Planning Board to oversee every sector of the economy. Chun's government directed investment away from capital-intensive chemical and heavy industries to the labor-intensive light industries that produced consumer goods. It curtailed excessive competition among *chaebol* by merging some of the *chaebol* subsidiaries engaged in similar ventures. The government also cut agricultural subsidies, sought to limit wage increases, and even declared cuts and a wage freeze in the state bureaucracy.

The economy began to improve in 1983. While South Korea had suffered a negative growth rate in 1980, it attained growth of 8.1% in 1983. Exports began picking up in mid-1983, and continued to gain strength. The upturn in the world economy and a good harvest in 1983 helped South Korea's economic situation. In that year the country attained its export target of $23.5 billion, a 7.6% increase over 1982. The consumer price index dropped from an average annual growth rate of 14.1% in the period from 1978 to 1982 to 2.9% in 1983–84.

The goals of Chun's government went beyond stabilization, however. The Chun regime drew the outlines of a reorientation of South Korean economic policy that would be further clarified and developed by Roh Tae Woo. One such goal was to redirect the economy into the manufacture of high-technology products—in particular, computers and computer components. Related to this new direction in developmental policy was the suggestion, reflecting a second change in government policy, that small, private enterprises would play a stronger role in these areas. This new orientation was part of a more general effort to lessen the role of government in the economy by creating a larger role for the private sector. Moreover, the government sought to limit the influence of the *chaebol* while promoting the growth of small- and medium-sized businesses by such methods as providing credit at favorable rates. Finally, there was talk of lowering South Korea's protectionist barriers by allowing greater foreign participation in the economy through imports, direct investment, and participation in the nation's financial markets.

On the face of it, these new policies seemed to be quite successful. Although GNP grew only 7% in 1985, the figures for the next three years registered 12.9%, 12.8%, and 12.2%. Wage raises following the strikes, the appreciation of the *won*, and the resulting decline in exports cut short the boom period as the growth rate plunged to 6.5% in 1989. A rebound in 1990 was abruptly halted when the Middle East crisis doubled the price of oil, bringing a downturn in the global economy. Since South Korea depends entirely on imported oil, and since it depends heavily on foreign trade, its economy will undoubtedly suffer if the crisis is not quickly resolved. But South Korean economists predict that the country will maintain a growth rate of 6.5% to 7% in 1991.

While overall growth was impressive, there was only halting progress toward the goals of reorientation formulated during the 1980's. First, the *chaebol* remain a dominant force in the South Korean economy. Despite the banks' instructions to make 35% of their loans to small- and medium-sized businesses, the huge conglomerates seem to have lost little influence. In 1984 the sales of the ten leading *chaebol* equaled two-thirds of South Korea's GNP. The sales of the top four equaled one-half of the national GNP in 1989. Moreover, despite constant talk of the need for the government to stop its direct management of the economy, it continues to intervene, leading one prominent economist in the ruling party to express the hope that in another five or ten years, market forces rather than the state will be guiding the economy. Finally, despite promises made to major industrial powers (particularly the United States), foreign participation in the South Korean economy, whether through trade, investment, or participation in financial institutions, remains quite restricted.

Future Prospects

South Korea has been aptly called a minidragon: its GNP in 1988 was only 18% and its total exports only 23% the value of Japan's. But it has earned a respectable place in the global economy during the past two decades because of its rapid growth in GNP and exports. In 1970 South Korea's exports totaled only slightly more than one-half of Taiwan's, which was behind Hong Kong and Singapore, but by 1980 South Korean exports nearly equaled those of the other three minidragons, and in 1988 exports exceeded those of both Singapore and Taiwan.

But what of the future? Will South Korea be able to maintain its rapid rate of growth? Will the country continue the process of democratization? What lies ahead in the relationship between North and South Korea?

In order to forecast the future of South Korea's economy, we must review some of the factors that contributed to past growth and analyze the challenges the country faces now. South Korea's rapid growth was facilitated by strong and stable political leadership motivated to bring about that growth; by the availability of an educated labor force; by the availability of capital and technology; and by a growing international market, particularly in the United States and Japan. The government also provided entrepreneurs with strong incentives and privileges, and it strictly controlled labor unions in order to enable exporters to compete successfully abroad.

Many of these conditions will remain, and thus can be expected to facilitate future growth, but others have changed or are in the process of changing. While South Korea will continue to offer an educated labor force, for example, entrepreneurs can no longer count on cheap labor to compete against foreign rivals. Not only is South Korean labor demanding higher wages, but many countries with lower wages, such as the People's Republic of China (PRC), are entering the international market; South Korea will find it impossible to compete. International markets have been changing also. While the depressed market of the early 1990's may recover its vigor in future years, South Korea must face the protectionist trend in the United

States and Europe. There is considerable impatience in these countries with the extremely slow pace at which the South Korean economy is opening to the outside world.

South Korean entrepreneurs have of course been exploring new markets. Radical changes in what used to be the communist bloc nations offer new opportunities. South Korea's trade with the Soviet Union and East European nations approached $1 billion in 1989 and is likely to increase. South Korea's trade with the PRC in the same year was over $3 billion. North Korea also offers considerable potential for trade in the future. While these new markets are small in comparison with those in the United States and Japan, and are fraught with dangers, South Koreans know that for future economic growth they must look beyond the economic superpowers.

Finally, South Korea must readjust the fundamentals of its economy in order to produce exports with higher domestic value added. To this end, South Korean entrepreneurs and pundits have been talking about the need to elevate the country's technological sophistication by investing more in research and development. Indeed, expenditures on research and development as a percentage of GNP have begun to rise rapidly. Since South Korea has no other choice for future growth but to increase its exports, it must refine its products and reduce the cost of production if it is to compete in the increasingly competitive market. The economic challenges are thus enormous.

The political picture is similarly one of great progress amid continuing challenges. In the summer of 1990, the British magazine *The Economist* praised what it called Roh Tae Woo's "huge gamble" for democracy, noting that

> [today,] by and large, Koreans are free to say and write what they think. Three years ago they were not. By and large, Korean workers get paid a wage that reflects their work. Three years ago they did not. Korea has not collapsed into an anarchy of petrol bombs and tear gas, as some feared it would. Nor has the army tried to take back the power it relinquished in 1987. Few countries with dictatorships so recent in their histories can boast as much.

There is surely something to be said for such an assessment. The loud complaints against the state of politics in South Korea today belie the sophistication and experience the society has gained since 1945. An educated population and a large middle class are important forces militating against any degeneration into chaos. Moreover, South Korea's relationship with North Korea has been improving over the past several years, with good prospects for stabilization. Finally, in the international realm, the government benefits from good relations with its old allies even as it establishes new ties with the changing socialist world.

Challenges remain, however. Political institutions remain fragile. So are the bonds that hold together the nation's elite; the powerful, unified state of the 1960's is no more. At the very top, South Korea's divided leaders must develop the art of compromise and consensus. Unlike earlier dictatorships, the South Korean government is no longer insulated from the demands of society. The outlines of interest group politics have been drawn as business, students, labor, and farmers all seek to shape government policies favorable to their demands and interests. Like its leaders, South Korean society must learn the art of compromise and consensus, even as its government is forced to learn the unfamiliar lessons of shaping policies amenable to competing social interests.

In short, as South Korea enters the 1990's, it faces a formidable agenda of political and economic challenges. Much has been accomplished, and much remains to be done. Yet in facing these challenges the South Korean people and their leaders will surely benefit from the self-confidence which they have gained during the past four decades, a period in which they prevailed over the seemingly enormous odds posed by national division and war.

Many South Koreans shared the gloomy prognosis General Helmick offered in 1948; at least they believed that they were doomed to live in poverty and dependency. Until the 1960's the South Koreans were not even certain that the capitalist system they espoused could effectively compete against communism. Since that time they have almost literally dug themselves up from poverty, and they now seem poised to join the ranks of the developed nations. South Korean products are recognized and respected throughout the world, and Roh Tae Woo's June 1990 meeting with Mikhail Gorbachev demonstrated the nation's growing international prestige. For the South Korean people, as well as for their government, the confidence and determination born of their past "miracles" may well be the crucial factors allowing them to surmount the formidable challenges ahead.

Page

Introduction

10   ***precisely what has occurred.*** This and the next two paragraphs are based on "The Pacific Rim, 1989," *Fortune* (January 20, 1990), pp. 74–82, Robert Wade; "What Can Economics Learn from East Asian Success?" *Annals of the American Academy of Political and Social Science,* Vol. 505 (September, 1989) p. 69; Lawrence B. Krause, "Changes in the International System: The Pacific Basin," *Ibid.,* p. 107; Lawrence Whitehead, "Tigers in Latin America?" *Ibid.,* pp. 142–51; Frederic Deyo, *Beneath the Miracle: Labor Subordination in the New Asian Industrialism* (Berkeley: University of California Press, 1989), Chap. 3, and Henry T. Oshima, "Human Resources in East Asia's Secular Growth," *Economic Development and Cultural Change,* Vol. 36, No. 3, Supplement (April, 1988), p. S104.

10   ***195% in Singapore.*** World Bank study cited in Whitehead, *Tigers,* p. 143. Export ratio from *The Economist, Book of Vital Statistics* (New York: Times Books, 1990), p. 155.

10   ***no domestic consumption of the products produced.*** Peter A. Gourevitch, "The Pacific Rim: Current Debates," *Annals of the American Academy of the Political and Social Science,* Vol. 505 (September, 1989), p. 19.

11   ***while reducing price distortions.*** Kuo-shu Liang and Ching-ing Hou Liang, "Development Policy Formation and Future Policy Priorities," *Economic Development and Cultural Change,* Vol. 36, No. 3, Supplement (April, 1988), pp. S71–72.

11   ***to have a limited lifespan.*** The remainder of this section is based on Deyo, *Beneath the Change,* pp. 23–37; Gary Rodan, *The Political Economy of Singapore's Industrialization: National, State and International Capital* (New York: St. Martin's Press, 1989), Chap. 5; Gary Gereffi, "Development Strategies and the Global Factory," *Annals of the American Academy of Political and Social Science,* Vol. 505 (September, 1989), pp. 92–104; Chung H. Lee and Seiji Naya, "Trade in East Asian Development with Comparative Reference to Southeast Asian Experiences," *Economic Development and Cultural Change,* Vol. 36, No. 3, Supplement (April, 1988), p. S129; and Alice Amsden, *Asia's Next Giant: South Korea and Late Industrialization* (New York: Oxford University Press, 1989), p. 154.

13   ***was instigated by the state.*** Amsden, *Asia's Next Giant,* p. 80.

13   ***involvement of government in direct production.*** This paragraph is based on Pang Eng Fang, "The Distinctive Features of Two States' Development: Hong Kong and Singapore," in Peter L. Berger and Hsin-Huang Michael Hsiao, *In Search of an East Asian Development Model* (New Brunswick, NJ: Transaction Books, 1988), p. 230; Lawrence B. Krause, "Hong Kong and Singapore: Twins or Kissing Cousins?", *Economic Development and Cultural Change,* Vol. 36, No. 3 (April, 1988), Supplement, pp. S45–S66; and Tun-jen Cheng and Stephan Haggard, *Newly Industrializing Asia in Transition* (Berkeley: Institute of International Studies, 1987), Chap. 5.

14   ***firms employed fewer than twenty persons.*** *The Economist* (July 14, 1990), p. 20.

14   ***precisely their undemocratic nature.*** Stephan Haggard and Chalmers Johnson have been among the most forceful exponents of the views developed in this paragraph and the next. See, for example, Stephan Haggard, "The East Asian NICs in Comparative Perspective," *Annals of the American Academy of Political and Social Science,* Vol. 505 (September, 1989), pp. 129–31, and Chalmers Johnson, "Political Institutions and Economic Performance," in Frederic Deyo, ed., *The Political Economy of the New East Asian Industrialism* (Ithaca: Cornell University Press, 1987), pp. 136–64.

15   ***make the market work better and faster.*** Krause, "Changes in the International System," p. 107.   A classic statement of this position can be found in Chalmers Johnson, *MITI and the Japanese Miracle* (Stanford: Stanford University Press, 1982).

15   ***can hardly be depicted as market-conforming.*** See, for example, Gordon White, ed., *Developmental States in East Asia* (New York: St. Martin's Press, 1988), and Amsden, *Asia's Next Giant,* Chap. 6.

15   ***two and one-half times that of the United States.*** Krause, "Changes in the International System," p. 109.

16   ***generated through banks in the colony.*** Deyo, *Beneath the Miracle,* p. 35.

16   ***53% of employment.*** Koh Ai Tee, "Linkages and the International Environment," in Lawrence B. Krause et al.,*The Singapore Economy Reconsidered* (Singapore: Institute of Southeast Asian Studies, 1987), Chap. 2.

16   ***debt as percentage of GNP grew from 0.8% to 7%.*** *Far Eastern Economic Review* (June 28, 1990), p. 44, and Amsden, *Asia's Next Giant,* p. 95.

16   ***those of the borrowers or lenders.*** This is a principal theme of the conclusion in Deyo, ed., *Political Economy.*

16   ***contributed to their past successes?*** This discussion has drawn from the summary of differing views in Gourevitch, *The Pacific Rim.*

16   ***the key to the "Eastasia edge."*** The book of this name places heavy emphasis on culture. See Roy Hofheinz, Jr. and Kent E. Calder, *The Eastasia Edge* (New York: Basic Books, 1982).

17   ***labor, landowners, and the bourgeoisie.*** This is an important theme of Haggard, "The East Asian NICs."

17   ***development of successful economic policies has been the international environment.*** This whole paragraph is based on Haggard.

17   ***"is without the means of its conservation."*** Quoted in Samuel P. Huntington, *Political Order in Changing Societies* (New Haven: Yale University Press, 1968), p. 19.

19   ***an end to tight government control.*** Cheng and Haggard, *Newly Industrializing Asia,* Chap. 6.

19   ***to unlearn the lessons of the past.*** Lawrence Krause cited in "South Korea: Survey," *The Economist* (August 18, 1990).

19   ***abstract notion of national economic growth.*** This discussion draws from the excellent treatment of the political implications of such social mobilization, see Haggard and Cheng, *Newly Industrializing Asia,* Chap. 6, and Stephan Haggard and Chung-in Moon, "Institutions and Economic Policy: Theory and a Korean Case Study," *World Politics,* Vol. 42, No. 2 (January, 1990), pp. 210–37.

21   ***took Western societies centuries to accomplish.*** On the issue of late industrialization, see Amsden, *Asia's Next Giant,* Chap. 1.

Taiwan

24   ***558 people per square kilometer.*** Council for Planning and Development, *Taiwan Statistical Data Yearbook,* 1990 (individual volumes of this annual cited hereafter as *TSDB*), p. 5.

25   ***join the global power elite.*** See Lewis H. Gann, "Western and Japanese Colonialism: Some Preliminary Comparisons," in Ramon Myers and Mark R. Peattie, eds., *The Japanese Colonial Empire, 1895–1945* (Princeton: Princeton University Press, 1984), pp. 497–525.

26   ***a significant proportion of the intellectual and social elite.*** The standard English work on this period is George Kerr, *Formosa Betrayed* (Boston: Houghton-Mifflin, 1965). With the unprecedented political opening of the mid-1980's, this once-taboo subject began to be discussed openly. See, e.g., Lin Qixu, *Taiwan Ererba Shijian: Zonghe Yanjiu* (Taiwan's 2.28: Comprehensive Research) (Kaohsiung: Xin Tai Zhenglun Zazhishe, n.d.).

27   ***a foundation for relatively equitable income distribution.*** On Taiwan's land reform, see Tang Hui-sun, *Land Reform in Free China* (Taipei: Joint Commission on Rural Reconstruction, 1954); Chen Cheng, *Land Reform in Taiwan* (Taipei: China Publishing Co., 1961); and Hsin-Huang Michael Hsiao, *Government Agricultural Strategies in Taiwan and South Korea* (Taipei: Academia Sinica, Institute of Ethnology, 1981).

28   ***40% of capital formation in Taiwan during the 1950's.*** K. T. Li, *The Evolution of Policy Behind Taiwan's Development Success* (New Haven: Yale University Press, 1988), p. 49. The most comprehensive study of American assistance is Neil H. Jacoby, *U. S. Aid to Taiwan* (New York: Praeger, 1966).

28   ***build an indigenous industrial base.*** Sources on this period include Ching-yuan Lin, *Industrialization in Taiwan, 1946–72* (New York: Praeger, 1973), and Samuel P. S. Ho, *Economic Development of Taiwan, 1860–1970* (New Haven: Yale University Press, 1978).

29   ***8.4% from 1973 to 1988.*** *TSDB, 1989,* p. 2.

29   ***approximately $7,500 in 1989.*** Ibid., p. 29, and *Free China Journal* (cited hereafter as *FCJ*) (August 27, 1990), p. 7.

29   ***hovering at 46% to 47% over the same period.*** *TSDB, 1990,* p. 41.

29   ***were other leading export items.*** Ibid., p. 213, and *TSDB, 1989,* pp. 227–28.

29   ***18.2% from 1973 to 1988.*** *TSDB, 1989,* p. 2.

29   ***figures for 1989 are 78.8% and 44%.*** 1952 and 1961 calculated from *TSDB, 1989,* pp. 26, 208; figures for 1989 from *FCJ* (August 27, 1989), p. 7.

29   ***$3,310 of which was exports.*** *TSDB, 1990,* p. 209.

29   ***has dominated government planning ever since.*** On the shift to export orientation, see M. Shahid Alam, *Governments and Markets in Economic Development Strategies: Lessons from Korea, Taiwan, and Japan* (New York: Praeger, 1989); Lin, *Taiwan Ererba Shijian;* Li, *Evolution of Policy;* and Maurice Scott, "Foreign Trade," in Walter Galenson, ed., *Economic Growth and Structural Change in Taiwan* (Ithaca: Cornell University Press, 1979), pp. 308–83.

31   **the huge trading firms in Japan and South Korea.** On reasons for the differences, see Karl J. Fields, "Trading Companies in South Korea and Taiwan: Two Policy Approaches," *Asian Survey*, Vol. 29, No. 11 (November, 1989), pp. 1073–89.

32   **on the central role of the state.** For the interaction of these forces see Thomas B. Gold, "Entrepreneurs, Multinationals and the State," in Edwin A. Winckler and Susan Greenhalgh, eds., *Contending Approaches to the Political Economy of Taiwan* (Armonk, NY: M.E. Sharpe, 1988), pp. 175–205.

49   **nearly all employees were family members.** For studies on Taiwanese entrepreneurship, see Hill Gates, "Dependency and the Part-Time Proletariat in Taiwan," *Modern China*, Vol. 5, No. 3 (July, 1979), pp. 381–408; Steven Harrell, "Why Do the Chinese Work So Hard?" *Modern China*, Vol. 11, No. 2 (April, 1985), pp. 203–26; Richard W. Stites, "Industrial Work as an Entrepreneurial Strategy," *Modern China*, Vol. 11, No. 2 (April, 1985), pp. 227–46.

49   **complex networks with other groups.** For two views on Taiwanese business, see Susan Greenhalgh, "Families and Networks in Taiwan's Economic Development," in Edwin A. Winckler and Susan Greenhalgh, eds., *Contending Approaches*, pp. 224–45, and Ichiro Numazaki, "Networks of Taiwanese Big Business," *Modern China*, Vol. 12, No. 4 (October, 1986), pp. 487–534.

49   **enterprises with fewer than fifty workers.** Gwo-shyong Shieh, *Manufacturing "Bosses": Subcontracting Networks under Dependent Capitalism in Taiwan*, Ph.D. diss., University of California, Berkeley, 1990, pp. 47, 49, Tables 2–3, 2–4.

50   **the emergence of an industrial working class.** The percentage of the labor force in industry rose from 16.9% in 1952 to 42.6% in 1988; 34.5% were in manufacturing (*TSDB, 1989*, p. 16). On labor, see Frederic Deyo, *Beneath the Miracle: Labor Subordination in the New Asian Industrialism* (Berkeley: University of California Press, 1990); Walter Galenson, "The Labor Force, Wages and Living Standards," in Walter Galenson, ed., *Economic Growth and Structural Change*, pp. 384–447; and Hill Gates, *Chinese Working-Class Lives* (Ithaca: Cornell University Press, 1987).

50   **outweigh the absolute investment figures.** A good overview can be found in Chi Schive, *The Foreign Factor: The Multinational Corporation's Contribution to the Economic Modernization of the Republic of China* (Stanford: Hoover Institution Press, 1990).

50   **(slightly over 6% in 1987).** Calculated from *TSDB, 1989*, pp. 54, 268. See also Gustav Ranis, "Industrial Development," in Walter Galenson, ed., *Economic Growth and Structural Change*, pp. 206–62.

51   **the major player in Taiwan's economy.** See, for example, Alice H. Amsden, "The State and Taiwan's Economic Development," in Peter B. Evans, Dietrich Rueschemeyer and Theda Skocpol, eds., *Bringing the State Back In* (New York: Cambridge University Press, 1985), pp. 78–106; Robert Wade, "What Can Economics Learn from East Asian Success?" *Annals of the American Academy of Political and Social Science*, Vol. 505 (September, 1989), pp. 68–79; and Stephan Haggard, "The East Asian NICs in Comparative Perspective,"*Ibid.*, pp. 129–41.

51   **market-oriented and indicative economic plans.** For further discussion of these concepts, see Chalmers Johnson, *MITI and the Japanese Miracle* (Stanford: Stanford University Press, 1982).

53   **began to give way at the end of the 1980's.** Two recent book-length studies of Taiwan's political evolution are Marc J. Cohen, *Taiwan at the Crossroads* (Washington, D.C.: Asia Resource Center, 1988), and Hung-mao Tien, *The Great Transition: Political and Social Change in the Republic of China* (Stanford: Hoover Institution Press, 1989). Two excellent articles are Tun-jen Cheng, "Democratizing the Quasi-Leninist Regime in Taiwan," *World Politics*, Vol. 41, No. 4 (July, 1989), pp. 471–99, and Yu-shan Wu, "Marketization of Politics: The Taiwan Experience," *Asian Survey*, Vol. 29, No. 4 (April, 1989), pp. 382–400.

53   **beyond the two-term limit.** This section is based on Tien, *The Great Transition*, pp. 108–12.

55   **without compelling the regime to liberalize.** For a glum view of Taiwanese politics, see Douglas Mendel, *The Politics of Formosan Nationalism* (Berkeley: University of California Press, 1970). For an analysis of American interests in Taiwan, see Ralph Clough, *Island China* (Cambridge: Harvard University Press, 1978).

55   **and were mutually reinforcing.** Two classic statements are Seymour Martin Lipset, "Some Social Requisites of Democracy: Economic Development and Political Legitimacy," *American Political Science Review*, Vol. 53 (March 1959), pp. 69–105, and Charles E. Lindblom, *Politics and Markets: The World's Political Systems* (New York: Basic Books, 1977).

55   **the uncertainties of democracy.** A collection of essays on this subject can be found in David Collier, ed., *The New Authoritarianism in Latin America* (Princeton: Princeton University Press, 1979).

56   **they formed a core of opposition.** See Chen Guu-ying, "The Reform Movement among Intellectuals in Taiwan Since 1970," *Bulletin of Concerned Asian Scholars*, Vol. 14, No. 3 (July–September, 1982), pp. 32–47, and Mab Huang, *Intellectual Ferment for Political Reforms in Taiwan, 1971–73* (Ann Arbor: Center for Chinese Studies, University of Michigan, 1976).

56   ***processes that raised pressures for democratization.*** Edwin A. Winckler, "Institutionalization and Participation on Taiwan: The Transition from Hard to Soft Authoritarianism?" *China Quarterly*, Vol. 99 (September, 1984), pp. 481–99.

59   ***Chiang died on January 13, 1988.*** For the events of 1988, see Thomas B. Gold, "Taiwan in 1988: The Transition to a Post-Chiang World," in Anthony J. Kane, ed., *China Briefing, 1989* (Boulder, CO: Westview Press, 1989), pp. 87–108.

59   ***stock market punters, and low-cost housing.*** For details, see Hsin-Huang Michael Hsiao, "Emerging Social Movements and the Rise of a Demanding Civil Society in Taiwan," *Australian Journal of Chinese Affairs*, Vol. 24 (July, 1990), pp. 163–79.

59   ***a question that made Beijing nervous.*** For the evolution of Beijing's policies toward Taiwan, see Wen Qing, "'One Country, Two Systems': The Best Way to Peaceful Reunification," *Beijing Review*, Vol. 33 (August 13–19, 1990), pp. 18–26.

62   ***reached US\$ 3.7 billion in 1989.*** *FCJ* (May 10, 1990), p. 2

62   ***passed US\$ 1 billion at the end of 1989.*** Elizabeth Cheng, "Taiwan Money One Bright Spot," *Far Eastern Economic Review* (August 23, 1990), p. 42.

Singapore

68   ***enjoyed by local industry in Taiwan and South Korea.*** Huang Chi, "The State and Foreign Investment: The Cases of Taiwan and Singapore," *Comparative Political Studies*, Vol. 22, No. 1 (April, 1989), pp. 93–121.

68   ***promotion of sports and recreational activities.*** Jon Quah, "The Public Bureaucracy in Singapore," in You Poh Seng and Lim Chong Yah, eds., *Singapore: Twenty-Five Years of Industrialization* (Singapore: Nan Yang Xing Zhou Lianhe Zabao).

69   ***achieving the highest savings rate in the world.*** Lawrence B. Krause, "Hong Kong and Singapore: Twins or Kissing Cousins?", *Economic Development and Cultural Change*, Vol. 36, No. 3, Supplement (April, 1988), pp. S45–S70.

69   ***160 local manufacturing and service sector companies.*** Linda Low, "Public Enterprises in Singapore," in You and Lim, *Singapore*.

69   ***shipping, finance and tourism.*** Krause, "Hong Kong and Singapore."

69   ***taxes on exports of approved products.*** Stephan Haggard, *Pathways from the Periphery* (Ithaca: Cornell University Press, 1990).

70   ***80% of total investment commitments in manufacturing.*** John Wong, "Transnational Corporations and Industrialization in Singapore," forthcoming in *Regional Development Dialogue*, 1990.

71   ***outranked tax and other industrial incentives.*** *Ibid.*

71   ***few such requirements on foreign investors.*** Huang Chi, "The State and Foreign Investment," p. 113.

71   ***cannot meet their quality and delivery requirements.*** Wong, "Transnational Corporations."

72   ***a number of Singapore's exports to the United States.*** Thomas J. Bellows, "Bridging Tradition and Modernization: The Singapore Bureaucracy," in Hungchao Tai, ed., *Confucianism and Economic Development: An Oriental Alternative?* (Washington, D.C.: The Washington Institute for Values in Public Policy, 1989), pp. 195–223.

72   ***78% in 1980 and 81% in 1988.*** N. Balakrishnan, "Battle of the Sexes," *Far Eastern Economic Review* (September 31, 1989), pp. 34–5.

73   ***increased from 19% to 28.4%.*** United Nations Economic and Social Commission for Asia and the Pacific, *Statistical Yearbook, 1988* (Bangkok: United Nations Economic and Social Commission for Asia and the Pacific,1988), p. 374.

75   ***textiles and other traditional labor-intensive industries.*** *Far Eastern Economic Review* (November 3, 1988), p. 115.

75   ***from 3.6% to 8.6% of total employment.*** Singapore Ministry of Labor cited in Krause, "Hong Kong and Singapore," p. S59.

75   ***worldwide restructuring in the mid-1980's.*** Sununta Siengthai, "Wages and Incomes Policy: The State Intervention in the Labor Market," unpublished manuscript (Bangkok: National Institute of Development Administration, 1990).

75   ***research and development activities in Singapore between 1980 and 1985.*** Wong, "Transnational Corporations."

75   *private funding only 92 million.* Statistical Yearbook, p. 374.

76   *overdependence on foreign investment.* Siengthai, "Wages and Incomes Policy," p. 24.

76   *the key to Singapore's economic growth.* Balakrishnan, "Battle of the Sexes," p. 74.

77   *the responsibility of the private sector.* Cited in Toh Mun Heng and Linda Low, "Economic Planning and Policy Making in Singapore," in *Economic Bulletin for Asia and the Pacific*, Vol. 39, No. 1 (June 1988), p. 28.

77   *the high technology they employ at home.* The Economist (June 9, 1990).

77   *"because they [had] lived longer."* Geoffrey Murray, "Is There Room for Genuine Political Opposition in Tiny Singapore?" *The Christian Science Monitor* (December 17, 1986).

78   *equal to New Zealand's.* Calculated from *Statistical Yearbook for Asia and the Pacific, 1988*, p. 362.

79   *employment near densely settled populations.* Janet Salaff, *State and Family in Singapore: Restructuring in an Industrial Society* (Ithaca: Cornell University Press, 1988).

80   *irresponsible parliamentary behavior.* Thomas Bellows, "Singapore in 1989: Progress in a Search for Roots," *Asian Survey*, Vol. 30, No. 2 (February, 1990), pp. 201–9.

80   *pronouncements of a political nature.* Barry Wilkinson, "Social Engineering in Singapore," *Journal of Contemporary Asia*, No. 2, (1988), p. 184.

97   *sells local souvenirs to visiting tourists.* Kenneth Roth, "Exiles in Disneyland," *Far Eastern Economic Review* (September 7, 1989), pp. 24–26.

97   *from access to public housing for five years.* Peter Chen, "Social Change and Planning in Singapore," in You and Lim, *Singapore: Twenty-Five Years of Industrialization*, p. 324.

98   *throwing trash out of housing estate windows.* Wilkinson, "Social Engineering."

98   *mass population in supporting Government policies.* Chen, "Social Change," in You and Lim, *Singapore: Twenty-Five Years of Industrialization*, p. 324.

98   *services to local community residents.* Bellows, "Bridging Tradition."

99   *jaywalkers over a recent twelve-month period.* U.S. News and World Report (October 15, 1990), p. 74.

99   *the nation will be no more.* The Economist (January 21, 1989), p. 33.

101   *couples with more than two children.* N. Balakrishnan, "Save as Your Spawn," *Far Eastern Economic Review* (May 17, 1990), pp. 52–54.

102   *union-supported wage restraint.* Ellen Salem, "Flexible Response: Singapore Attempts to Appease Its Discontented Workforce," *Far Eastern Economic Review* (September 8, 1988), p. 141.

102   *development policy in an increasingly complex economy.* Krause, "Hong Kong and Singapore."

103   *I'll get up.* New York Times (November 6, 1990), p. A4.

Hong Kong

106   *its principal function has been as a base for trade.* Norman J. Miners, *The Government and Politics of Hong Kong*, 4th ed. (Hong Kong: Oxford University Press, 1986), p. 15.

106   *37% of its exports passed through the territory.* G. B. Endicott, *A History of Hong Kong*, 2nd ed. (Hong Kong: Oxford University Press, 1987), p. 253.

106   *38% of its imports involved trade with China.* Edward Szczepanik, *The Economic Growth of Hong Kong* (London: Oxford University Press, 1958), p. 58. Disaggregation of exports and re-exports is unavailable for these years.

107   *involved the government in land management.* Ian Scott, *Political Change and the Crisis of Legitimacy in Hong Kong* (Hong Kong: Oxford University Press, 1989), Chap. 2.

107   *to uphold and enforce Confucian morality and virtues.* Lau Siu-kai and Kuan Hsin-chi, *The Ethos of the Hong Kong Chinese* (Hong Kong: Chinese University Press, 1988), p. 34.

107   *but excluded everyone else.* Scott, *Political Change*, Chap. 2.

107   *unconcerned with human feelings, hidebound and aloof.* Lau and Kuan, *Ethos of the Hong Kong Chinese*, p. 22.

108   *pre-industrial society with no very evident future.* A. J. Youngson, *Hong Kong: Economic Growth and Policy* (Hong Kong: Oxford University Press, 1982), p. 2.

108   ***mainland Chinese were attracted to Hong Kong.*** Wong Siu-lun, *Emigrant Entrepreneurs: Shanghai Industrialists in Hong Kong* (Hong Kong: Oxford University Press, 1988), p. 19. The Nationalist Party (KMT), nationalized 40% of the country's spindleage in 1946, rationed industrial raw materials like cotton, introduced price and distribution controls, and prohibited private holdings in foreign exchange.

108   ***spindles installed in Hong Kong rose from 6,000 to 180,000.*** Youngson, *Hong Kong* , p. 3.

108   ***cannot be overestimated.*** See Stephan Haggard and Cheng Tun-jen, "State and Foreign Capital in the East Asian NICs," in Frederic Deyo, ed., *The Political Economy of the New East Asian Industrialism* (Ithaca: Cornell University Press, 1987), p. 107.

108   ***refugees were arriving in Hong Kong every week.*** Szczepanik, *Economic Growth*, p. 154.

108   ***goods from the West and Japan for sale in China.*** Ibid., pp. 54–55.

108   ***only 60,000 to 70,000 people were employed in manufacturing.*** Youngson, *Hong Kong*, p. 3.

109   ***dwindling to HK$ 136 million in 1956.*** Szczepanik, *Economic Growth*, p. 158.

109   ***incentive to concentrate on exports from the beginning.*** Edward K. Y. Chen, "The Newly Industrializing Countries of Asia: Growth Experience and Prospects," in Robert A. Scalapino, Seizaburo Sato, and Jusuf Wanandi, eds., *Asian Economic Development—Present and Future* (Berkeley: Institute of East Asian Studies, 1985), p. 137.

109   ***ultimately found its way to Hong Kong.*** Citing Parks Coble, *The Shanghai Capitalists and the Nationalist Government* (Cambridge: Harvard University Press, 1980), in Haggard and Cheng, "State and Foreign Capital," p. 89.

109   ***9.2% during the decade.*** The World Bank, *World Tables, Volume 1: Economic Data from the Files of the World Bank*, 3rd. ed. (Baltimore: Johns Hopkins University Press, 1983), p. 488.

109   ***consistent annual growth rates of more than 10%.*** K. R. Chou, *The Hong Kong Economy: A Miracle of Growth* (Hong Kong: Academic Publications, 1966), p. 81. See also Chou's discussion of the problems of measuring GDP during the period.

109   ***a world economic recession in 1974–75.*** See Edward K. Y. Chen, "The Economic Setting," in David G. Lethbridge, ed., *The Business Environment in Hong Kong*, 2nd ed. (Hong Kong: Oxford University Press, 1984), pp. 4–7.

110   ***at a rate of 1:7.8.*** Y. C. Jao, "Hong Kong's Future as a Free Market Economy," *Issues and Studies* (June, 1986), p. 117.

110   ***increased by almost 60% to 145,000.*** Szczepanik, *Economic Growth*, p. 159. In 1954, industrial workers made up about 11.2% of the working age population.

110   ***the territory's largest employer.*** E. K. Y. Chen, "The Economic Setting," in D. G. Lethbridge, ed., *The Business Environment in Hong Kong*, 2nd ed. (Hong Kong: Oxford University Press, 1984), pp. 9 and 16.

111   ***employed only about 30% of the work force.*** *Hong Kong, 1990* (Hong Kong: Government Printer, 1990), p. 99.

111   ***for the first time in 1980.*** Chen, "The Economic Setting," p. 8. Chen notes that the very high level of financial services, contribution to GDP in the early 1960's was due to a real estate boom, rather than to growth of services of banks and other financial institutions.

111   ***more recently, watches and clocks.*** Textiles' share of all manufacturing has fallen from 29% in 1973 to 18.2% in 1985, while electronics have increased substantially from 11% in 1973 to more than 20% in 1983. See Edward K. Y. Chen and K. W. Li, "Industry," in H. C. Y. Ho and L. C. Chau, eds., *The Economic System of Hong Kong* (Hong Kong: Asian Research Service, 1988), p. 115.

111   ***71% of its total exports.*** *Hong Kong 1990* (Hong Kong: Government Printer, 1990), p. 78.

111   ***were destined for the American market.*** Chen, "The Economic Setting," p. 29; *Hong Kong, 1985* (Hong Kong: Hong Kong Government Printer, 1985), p. 308; and *Hong Kong, 1990* (Hong Kong: Government Printer, 1990), p. 389.

111   ***have imposed similar restrictions.*** See Chen, "The Economic Setting," pp. 25–27, and Cheng Tong Yung, *The Economy of Hong Kong* (Hong Kong: Far East Publications, 1977), pp. 184–85.

112   ***only about one-third those in Hong Kong.*** Victor F. S. Sit, "Hong Kong's New Industrial Partnership with the Pearl River Delta," *Asian Geographer*, Vol. 8, Nos. 1 and 2 (1989), p. 108.

112   ***2.5 million workers across the border.*** *Dagong bao* (Hong Kong, July 9, 1989).

112   ***increase in trade between the two countries.*** E. K. Y. Chen, "The Impact of China's Four Modernizations on Hong Kong's Economic Development," in A. J. Youngson, ed., *China and Hong Kong: The Economic Nexus* (Hong Kong: Oxford University Press), p. 89; *Hong Kong, 1987* (Hong Kong: Hong Kong Government Printer, 1987), p. 321; and *Hong Kong, 1990*, p. 389.

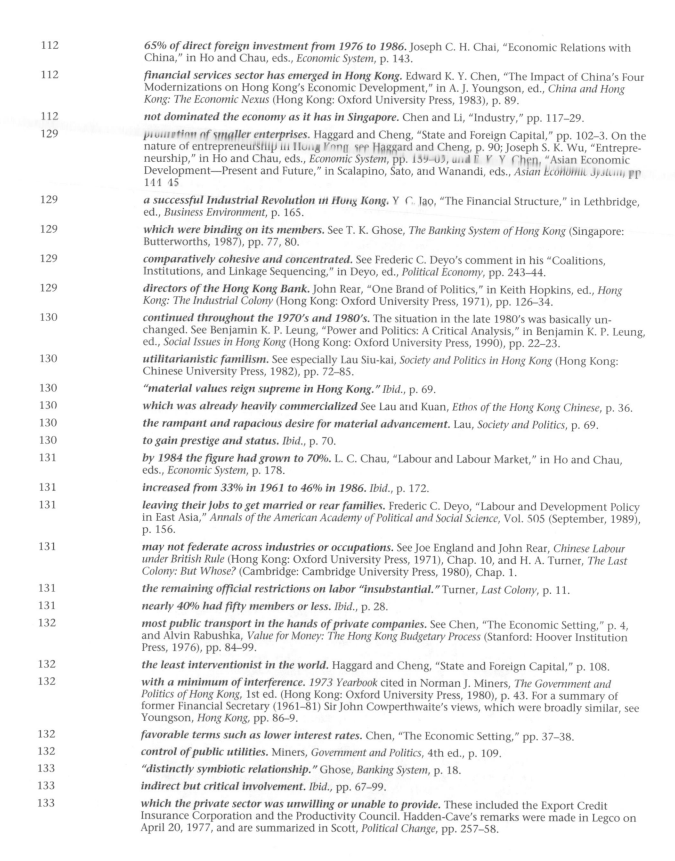

112   *65% of direct foreign investment from 1976 to 1986.* Joseph C. H. Chai, "Economic Relations with China," in Ho and Chau, eds., *Economic System*, p. 143.

112   *financial services sector has emerged in Hong Kong.* Edward K. Y. Chen, "The Impact of China's Four Modernizations on Hong Kong's Economic Development," in A. J. Youngson, ed., *China and Hong Kong: The Economic Nexus* (Hong Kong: Oxford University Press, 1983), p. 89.

112   *not dominated the economy as it has in Singapore.* Chen and Li, "Industry," pp. 117–29.

129   *promotion of smaller enterprises.* Haggard and Cheng, "State and Foreign Capital," pp. 102–3. On the nature of entrepreneurship in Hong Kong see Haggard and Cheng, p. 90; Joseph S. K. Wu, "Entrepreneurship," in Ho and Chau, eds., *Economic System*, pp. 139–03, and E. K. Y. Chen, "Asian Economic Development—Present and Future," in Scalapino, Sato, and Wanandi, eds., *Asian Economic System*, pp. 144–45

129   *a successful Industrial Revolution in Hong Kong.* Y. C. Jao, "The Financial Structure," in Lethbridge, ed., *Business Environment*, p. 165.

129   *which were binding on its members.* See T. K. Ghose, *The Banking System of Hong Kong* (Singapore: Butterworths, 1987), pp. 77, 80.

129   *comparatively cohesive and concentrated.* See Frederic C. Deyo's comment in his "Coalitions, Institutions, and Linkage Sequencing," in Deyo, ed., *Political Economy*, pp. 243–44.

129   *directors of the Hong Kong Bank.* John Rear, "One Brand of Politics," in Keith Hopkins, ed., *Hong Kong: The Industrial Colony* (Hong Kong: Oxford University Press, 1971), pp. 126–34.

130   *continued throughout the 1970's and 1980's.* The situation in the late 1980's was basically unchanged. See Benjamin K. P. Leung, "Power and Politics: A Critical Analysis," in Benjamin K. P. Leung, ed., *Social Issues in Hong Kong* (Hong Kong: Oxford University Press, 1990), pp. 22–23.

130   *utilitarianistic familism.* See especially Lau Siu-kai, *Society and Politics in Hong Kong* (Hong Kong: Chinese University Press, 1982), pp. 72–85.

130   *"material values reign supreme in Hong Kong."* Ibid., p. 69.

130   *which was already heavily commercialized* See Lau and Kuan, *Ethos of the Hong Kong Chinese*, p. 36.

130   *the rampant and rapacious desire for material advancement.* Lau, *Society and Politics*, p. 69.

130   *to gain prestige and status.* Ibid., p. 70.

131   *by 1984 the figure had grown to 70%.* L. C. Chau, "Labour and Labour Market," in Ho and Chau, eds., *Economic System*, p. 178.

131   *increased from 33% in 1961 to 46% in 1986.* Ibid., p. 172.

131   *leaving their jobs to get married or rear families.* Frederic C. Deyo, "Labour and Development Policy in East Asia," *Annals of the American Academy of Political and Social Science*, Vol. 505 (September, 1989), p. 156.

131   *may not federate across industries or occupations.* See Joe England and John Rear, *Chinese Labour under British Rule* (Hong Kong: Oxford University Press, 1971), Chap. 10, and H. A. Turner, *The Last Colony: But Whose?* (Cambridge: Cambridge University Press, 1980), Chap. 1.

131   *the remaining official restrictions on labor "insubstantial."* Turner, *Last Colony*, p. 11.

131   *nearly 40% had fifty members or less.* Ibid., p. 28.

132   *most public transport in the hands of private companies.* See Chen, "The Economic Setting," p. 4, and Alvin Rabushka, *Value for Money: The Hong Kong Budgetary Process* (Stanford: Hoover Institution Press, 1976), pp. 84–99.

132   *the least interventionist in the world.* Haggard and Cheng, "State and Foreign Capital," p. 108.

132   *with a minimum of interference.* 1973 Yearbook cited in Norman J. Miners, *The Government and Politics of Hong Kong*, 1st ed. (Hong Kong: Oxford University Press, 1980), p. 43. For a summary of former Financial Secretary (1961–81) Sir John Cowperthwaite's views, which were broadly similar, see Youngson, *Hong Kong*, pp. 86–9.

132   *favorable terms such as lower interest rates.* Chen, "The Economic Setting," pp. 37–38.

132   *control of public utilities.* Miners, *Government and Politics*, 4th ed., p. 109.

133   *"distinctly symbiotic relationship."* Ghose, *Banking System*, p. 18.

133   *indirect but critical involvement.* Ibid., pp. 67–99.

133   *which the private sector was unwilling or unable to provide.* These included the Export Credit Insurance Corporation and the Productivity Council. Hadden-Cave's remarks were made in Legco on April 20, 1977, and are summarized in Scott, *Political Change*, pp. 257–58.

133   *a government has to in difficult circumstances.* "Preface," in Lethbridge, ed., *Business Environment.*

133   *to put the deal[s] together.* Ghose, *Banking System,* p. 97.

134   *to assist industry to become more competitive.* Miners, *The Government and Politics,* 4th ed., pp. 106–7.

134   *the provision of financial services.* See Chen, "The Economic Setting," pp. 44-46.

134   *prevented landlords from evicting sitting tenants. Ibid.,* p. 38.

135   *would redistribute benefits to alienated groups.* This account draws heavily on Scott, *Political Changes,* Chaps. 2–4.

135   *a new structure of authority. Ibid.,* p. 59.

135   *attacks on the police. Ibid.,* p. 92.

136   *strong links to the procommunist Federation of Trade Unions. Ibid.,* pp. 98–106.

136   *to rule with the consent of the people. Ibid.,* p. 105.

137   *increased by 65.5%, from 104,876 to 173,633.* John P. Burns and Ian Scott, "A Profile of the Civil Service," in Ian Scott and John P. Burns, eds., *The Hong Kong Civil Service Personnel Policies and Practices* (Hong Kong: Oxford University Press, 1984), p. 17.

137   *to a high of 19.2% in 1982–83.* H. C. Y. Ho, "Public Finance," in Ho and Chau, eds., *Economic System,* p. 18.

137   *restrict the growth of the civil service.* See N. C. Owen, "Economic Policy," in Keith Hopkins, ed., *Hong Kong: The Industrial Colony* (Hong Kong: Oxford University Press, 1971), p. 155.

137   *signed the Sino-British joint declaration on the future of Hong Kong.* See the "Joint Declaration of the Government of the United Kingdom of Great Britain and Northern Ireland and the Government of the People's Republic of China on the Question of Hong Kong," 1984.

137   *"Hong Kong people will govern Hong Kong."* See Annex 1 to the Joint Declaration, in which China elaborates its policies for the future government of the special administrative region.

137   *confidence in both the agreement and the Hong Kong government.* See Scott, *Political Change,* Chap. 5.

138   *would go into 1997 without any agreement at all.* See "A Draft Agreement Between the Government of the United Kingdom of Great Britain and Northern Ireland and the Government of the People's Republic of China on the Future of Hong Kong" (Hong Kong: Hong Kong Government Printer, 1984), p. 7.

138   *accepted the agreement as better than nothing.* See Report of the Assessment Office, *Submissions Made by Organizations to the Assessment Office,* Vols. I and II (Hong Kong: Hong Kong Government Printer, 1984).

138   *freedoms of the press and association.* These are reported in Joseph Y. S. Cheng, *Hong Kong: In Search of a Future* (Hong Kong: Oxford University Press, 1984).

138   *became a lame duck.* See Chief Secretary Sir David Ford's comments in Legco, November 5, 1987, in Scott, *Political Change,* p. 280.

138   *reactions of strategic groups in Hong Kong varied.* See John P. Burns, "The Process of Assimilation of Hong Kong (1997) and the Implications for Taiwan," *AEI Foreign Policy and Defense Review,* Vol. 6, No. 3 (1986), pp. 19–26.

138   *seemed to undermine the territory's autonomy.* The "Basic Law of the Hong Kong Special Administrative Region of the People's Republic of China" was promulgated in April, 1990.

138   *promised a more representative government for Hong Kong.* British Foreign Secretary Sir Geoffrey Howe's press conference in Hong Kong, *South China Morning Post* (Hong Kong, April 21, 1984).

139   *99% of the population of Hong Kong were excluded from voting.* See Scott, *Political Change,* Chap. 7.

139   *the Basic Law governing post–1997 Hong Kong.* See Martin Lee and Szeto Wah, *The Basic Law: Some Basic Flaws* (Hong Kong: Kasper Printing Co., 1988).

139   *people are likely to have moved overseas.* This was the Hong Kong government's estimate. See *South China Morning Post* (Hong Kong, May 8, 1990).

140   *relegate Hong Kong to a subregional role.* Miron Mushkat, *The Economic Future of Hong Kong* (Boulder: Lynne Rienner Publishers, 1990), pp. 143–49.

140   *US$ 300 million was invested in manufacturing.* Joseph C. H. Chai, "Economic Relations with China," in Ho and Chau, eds, *Economic System,* p. 143, and Hong Kong Government Industry Department, *The 1989 Survey of Overseas Investment in Hong Kong's Manufacturing Industries* (Hong Kong: Industry Department, 1990), p. 70.

140   **the Eastern Cross Harbour Tunnel.** *South China Morning Post* (Hong Kong, March 23, 1990).

142   **chosen indirectly by the CCP.** According to the Basic Law, the Selection Committee will be chosen by a Preparatory Committee, which in turn is selected by the Standing Committee of the National People's Congress (NPC) in Beijing. However, the selection of the Standing Committee of the NPC is approved by the Chinese Communist Party (CCP), its agenda is fixed by the CCP, and it is convened only on the instructions of the CCP Politburo. Consequently, this means that the local CCP in Hong Kong (the Hong Kong and Macau Work Committee) will draw up the list of names of the Preparatory Committee and pass it on to the Standing Committee of the NPC for ratification. The CCP-approved Preparatory Committee will then choose the Selection Committee. Indirectly, then, the CCP will determine Hong Kong's first legislature and chief executive. See "The Basic Law," Annex I and II, and "Decision of the National People's Congress on the Method for the Formation of the First Government and the First Legislative Council of the Hong Kong Special Administrative Region" (April, 1990).

142   **now rate that factor as unfavorable.** Hong Kong Government Industry Department, *1989 Survey*, p. 56. According to this survey, the four most important factors determining the extent to which Hong Kong has a favorable investment climate were: political stability, political future, banking and financial facilities, and infrastructure (in that order). See p. 54.

142   **20% of the PRC's net foreign exchange.** Joseph C. H. Chai, "Economic Relations with China," pp. 140–43. Chai notes that from 1979 to 1984 China's gross foreign exchange earnings from Hong Kong were about 30%, while net earnings were about 20%.

South Korea

144   **nonfood producers would face starvation.** *Foreign Relations of the United States*, 1948, Vol. VI, p. 1092.

145   **has risen from fifty-eight to seventy years.** *The Economist*, July 14, 1990, p. 19. For a discussion of South Korea's educational system, see Alice Amsden, *Asia's Next Giant: South Korea and Late Industrialization* (New York: Oxford University Press, 1989), Chap. 9.

145   **competition with the Communist North.** On "international shocks" see Stephan Haggard, "The East Asian NICs in Comparative Perspective," *Annals of the American Academy of Political and Social Science*, Vol. 505 (September 1989), pp. 129–141.

147   **had fallen from its 1910 level by nearly half.** From Chong-Sik Lee, *Japan and Korea: The Political Dimension* (Stanford: Stanford University Press, 1985).

148   **less than 1% had finished middle school.** Chosen Sotokufu (Korean Government-General), *Jinko chosa kekka hokoku* (Report on the Result of the Population Census), May 1, 1944, Pt. 2, pp. 142–43. The report indicated that 11.65% of males graduated from elementary school, while 3.01% of females did so. An additional 1.11% of the population had attended elementary school but did not graduate. The percentage of children ages 7–14 attending school as of 1935 was 17.59% (27.26% male and 7.33% female). See Chosen Ko-sei Kyokai (Korean Welfare Association), *Chosen ni okeru jinko ni kansurusho tokei* (Various Statistics Concerning Population in Korea) (Seoul, 1943), p. 114.

149   **of the total industrial output of Korea.** George M. McCune, *Korea Today* (Cambridge: Harvard University Press, 1950), p. 158.

150   **twice as much in value as their economic aid.** Hagen Koo, "The Interplay of State, Social Class, and World System in East Asian Development The Cases of South Korea and Taiwan," in Frederic Deyo, *The Political Economy of the New East Asian Industrialism* (Ithaca: Cornell University Press, 1987), p. 168.

151   **the United States and the UN Reconstruction Agency.** The first annual United States economic aid bill after the armistice came to $200 million; it rose to a peak of $365 million in 1956, and never went below $200 million annually until nearly the mid-1960's. The South Korean government budget became dependent on such aid not only for defense, but for other expenditures as well. The level of budget assistance from foreign aid grew from a third of the total budget in 1954 to 58.4% in 1956; it was still at 38% in 1960. See David Cole and Princeton Lyman, *Korean Development: The Interplay of Politics and Economics* (Cambridge: Harvard University Press, 1971), p. 22.

151   **the wisdom of its import substituting development strategy.** Frederic Deyo, *Beneath the Miracle: Labor Subordination in the New East Asian Industrialism* (Berkeley: University of California Press, 1989), pp. 16–17.

154   **$416 million in government loans between 1965 and 1973.** Economic Planning Board, Republic of Korea, *Major Statistics of the Korean Economy*, 1977 (Seoul, 1977), pp. 200–205, and *Oegukin t'uja paekso* (White Paper on investment by Foreign Nationals) (Seoul, 1981), pp. 126–29, 136–37.

155   *increased to 44.5% in 1963 and 73.5% in 1968.* Cole and Lyman, *Korean Development*, p. 160. For another excellent overview of South Korea's economic development, see Edward D. Mason et al., *The Economic and Social Modernization of the Republic of Korea* (Cambridge, MA: 1980). Chapter 5 deals with industrialization and foreign trade. See also Wontack Hong and Anne O. Krueger, eds., *Trade and Development in Korea* (Seoul, 1975), passim.

155   *in particular, textiles, clothing, and footware.* Gary Gereffi, "Developmental Strategies in the Global Factory," *Annals of the American Academy of Political and Social Science*, Vol. 505 (September 1989), p. 101.

155   *the actual rate was near 30%.* Dong-a Ilbo (September 7, 1971). For a comprehensive diagnosis of the South Korean economy based on interviews with numerous economists, business leaders, and government officials, see a series of articles published in *ibid.*, April 10–28, 1979, under the title "Sixteen Years of Excess Growth: Korean Economy under Amber Signal." An abridgement of this series is published in Japanese translation in *Korea Hyoron* (Korean Review, Tokyo, August and September, 1979), pp. 43–53, 1423.

156   *the government party's share declined to 30.9%.* For details, see C. I. Eugene Kim, "Significance of Korea's 10th National Assembly Election," *Asian Survey*, Vol. 19, No. 5 (May, 1979), pp. 523–32.

157   *launched a scathing attack against the policies of the Park government.* Minju Chonson (Democratic Front), organ of the NDP (July 23, 1979).

177   *the formation of a new coalition party.* This paragraph is based on *The Far Eastern Economic Review*, June 29, 1990, p. 37.

179   *began to improve in 1983.* This paragraph and the next are based on Tun-jen Cheng and Stephan Haggard, *Newly Industrializing Asia in Transition* (Berkeley: Institute of International Studies, 1987), Chap. 2.

179   *registered 12.9%, 12.8%, and 12.2%.* From Bank of Korea, *Monthly Bulletin*, various issues.

179   *a growth rate of 6.5% to 7% in 1991.* Choson Ilbo (November 4, 1990).

179   *the goals of reorientation formulated during the 1980's.* This entire paragraph is based on *The Economist*, July 14, 1990, pp. 19–22.

181   *$1 billion in 1989 and is likely to increase.* South Korea's trade with the Soviet Union in 1989 was $599,446,000. Its trade with East European nations was $388,473,000. Trade with China was $3,141,895,000. *Maeil kyongje shinmun* (Daily Economic News, Seoul, March 23, 1990).

181   *can boast as much.* "Survey: South Korea," *The Economist*, August 19, 1990, p. 5.